New Directions for
Adult and Continuing
Education

Susan Imel
Jovita M. Ross-Gordon
COEDITORS-IN-CHIEF

MW01598767

Transnational Migration, Social Inclusion, and Adult Education

Shibao Guo
Elizabeth Lange
EDITORS

Number 146 • Summer 2015
Jossey-Bass
San Francisco

TRANSNATIONAL MIGRATION, SOCIAL INCLUSION, AND ADULT EDUCATION
Shibao Guo, Elizabeth Lange (eds.)
New Directions for Adult and Continuing Education, no. 146
Susan Imel, Jovita M. Ross-Gordon, Coeditors-in-Chief

Microfilm copies of issues and articles are available in 16mm and 35mm, as well as microfiche in 105mm, through University Microfilms Inc., 300 North Zeeb Road, Ann Arbor, Michigan 48106-1346.

NEW DIRECTIONS FOR ADULT AND CONTINUING EDUCATION (ISSN 1052-2891, electronic ISSN 1536-0717) is part of The Jossey-Bass Higher and Adult Education Series and is published quarterly by Wiley Subscription Services, Inc., A Wiley Company, at Jossey-Bass, One Montgomery Street, Suite 1200, San Francisco, CA 94104-4594. POSTMASTER: Send address changes to New Directions for Adult and Continuing Education, Jossey-Bass, One Montgomery Street, Suite 1200, San Francisco, CA 94104-4594.

New Directions for Adult and Continuing Education is indexed in CIJE: Current Index to Journals in Education (ERIC); Contents Pages in Education (T&F); ERIC Database (Education Resources Information Center); Higher Education Abstracts (Claremont Graduate University); and Sociological Abstracts (CSA/CIG).

INDIVIDUAL SUBSCRIPTION RATE (in USD): $89 per year US/Can/Mex, $113 rest of world; institutional subscription rate: $335 US, $375 Can/Mex, $409 rest of world. Single copy rate: $29. Electronic only–all regions: $89 individual, $335 institutional; Print & Electronic–US: $98 individual, $402 institutional; Print & Electronic–Canada/Mexico: $98 individual, $442 institutional; Print & Electronic–Rest of World: $122 individual, $476 institutional.

EDITORIAL CORRESPONDENCE should be sent to the Coeditors-in-Chief, Susan Imel, 3076 Woodbine Place, Columbus, Ohio 43202-1341, e-mail: imel.l@osu.edu; or Jovita M. Ross-Gordon, Southwest Texas State University, CLAS Dept., 601 University Drive, San Marcos, TX 78666.

Cover design: Wiley
Cover Images: © Lava 4 images | Shutterstock

www.josseybass.com

CONTENTS

EDITORS' NOTES

Migration has been a persistent element in human history, yet the rates of migration have reached historical peak numbers. The nature of migration has also changed as migrants are often transnational, maintaining strong ties to their country of origin as well as the new host country. This human mobility is influencing the fabric of many countries through increased diversity, prompting dialogues about citizenship rights and responsibilities, social justice, and community inclusion. Further, the causes of migration now often relate to transborder injustices and forced displacement—from climate change, disease, predatory capital, and global recession to extremist terror.

Historically, adult education has been related to immigration. In settler nations such as Canada, Australia, Aotearoa/New Zealand, and the United States, immigration has been used for nation building, industrialization, border protection, and economic growth. Early 20th-century adult education often sought to catalyze social reform, build citizenship capacity, and enhance workplace skills through learning, enabling new populations to integrate successfully into the daily social and economic life of the adopted country. In Europe, more jobs than local workers during the post–World War II boom led to many countries recruiting workers from former colonies, part of the "pull" factors of immigration. Today, the economic disparity across the globe has also created "push" factors, as citizens of the Global South seek out enhanced economic and educational opportunities in the Global North. For involuntary migrants, conflict, persecution, or environmental disaster compels them to seek refuge in another country.

In the 20th century social welfare state, the education needs of adult newcomers have been met by programs offering basic education, language, literacy, skills training, and professional education. These programs have been developed by various funders and providers—the state, educational institutions, nongovernmental organizations (NGOs), and ethnocultural community organizations. Yet, until recently, there has been a lack of interest among adult educators who do not work in settlement and immigrant-related programs. This New Directions volume seeks to inform the growing interest among adult educators.

The high level of global migration is considered a consequence of neoliberal globalization economics and expanding industrialization, generating growing global inequality. In the previous century, migration was often one way, with family members unsure they would see each other again. However, with the growing ease of global communication and transportation, the mobility of people within (rural to urban) and across national boundaries has accelerated and migrants now maintain strong ties to their origin and host countries, or constantly circulate as in the European Union. Enriching the multicultural fabric of societies, immigrants most often create more

NEW DIRECTIONS FOR ADULT AND CONTINUING EDUCATION, no. 146, Summer 2015 © 2015 Wiley Periodicals, Inc.
Published online in Wiley Online Library (wileyonlinelibrary.com) • DOI: 10.1002/ace.20126

jobs than they take and pay more in taxes than they take in welfare services (Organisation for Economic Co-operation and Development, 2013). Remittances also flow from migrants back to source regions and countries, bringing economic and educational advantages globally. Yet, too often, fear and suspicion underlies responses to immigrant populations.

Although immigration has long been used to ameliorate labor shortages and aging populations, migration policies are now a competition for the most talented, educated, and skillful. Nevertheless, the dynamics tend toward deskilling, where lack of credential recognition creates a downward mobility of well-educated migrants. Migrant flow now increasingly includes seasonal workers and longer term contract workers who move according to agricultural seasons and the fortunes of resource industries. These temporary foreign workers now outnumber permanent immigrants in some countries, but opportunities for exploitation also increase. Despite famine and the increasing number of conflict zones, environmental reasons now top the causes for seeking refugee status, largely related to climate change and sea level rise.

The United Nations now estimates that 232 million of the world's population lives outside the country of their birth. The foreign-born population within the Organisation for Economic Co-operation and Development (OECD) countries reached 12.5% of total populations in 2011, with Australia leading this group with 26.8% of its citizens being foreign born, followed by Canada at 20.6%, Germany at 13%, the United States at 12.9%, and the United Kingdom at 11.5% (OECD, 2013). When migrants arrive in a new society, they bring their values, language, culture, and ways of knowing, contributing significantly to the diversity of host countries. Many migrants also return home as conditions change, importing new ideas and practices into their countries of origin. These global demographic, social, and cultural changes create new opportunities and challenges for practices of social inclusion, particularly in adult education. Yet, since the 9/11 attacks in the United States, there has also been an increase in restrictive securitization policies, racial profiling, refugee deterrence, and reduced settlement services. Thus, multileveled social justice issues permeate immigration dynamics and challenge adult educators to rethink social justice in a transnational age. To do this, adult educators need to understand the complexities of migration and immigration, and reconstitute educational practices that can expand justice, social inclusion, community resilience, and reciprocal integration.

This volume of *New Directions for Adult and Continuing Education* examines the changing nature of adult education in the age of transnational migration, including the latest research, policies, and practices. It consists of nine chapters that generally follow the migration trajectory. The final three chapters (Chapters 7, 8, and 9) examine the larger historical and structural issues of race and gender in immigration and newer theories, such as diaspora studies, in relation to adult education. Nancy Fraser's (2009) concepts of *redistributive, recognitive,* and *representational justice* are threaded throughout the volume.

In Chapter 1, Shibao Guo describes transnational migration, mapping the contemporary dynamics and theorizing some of the complexities that characterize it. He then turns his attention to four issues related to the adult education field—the devaluation of foreign credentials, the marginalization of immigrant women and ways they still mobilize their prior knowledge and expertise, the value and danger of volunteering and informal learning, and the role of ethnocultural organizations as spaces and places for adult education. He proposes a paradigm shift toward recognitive adult education, which expands the concept of social justice beyond Eurocentric ideas.

In Chapter 2, Hongxia Shan begins with a historical overview of immigrant settlement services, using Canada as an exemplar. She profiles the ideological shift from assimilation to integration across many countries and she provides examples of this shift within adult education programs. She argues that although integration may be a goal, the practice of it is difficult and often contradictory. She advocates for a participatory mode of governance where immigrants participate in the design and delivery of settlement services, particularly training and education. She proposes moving beyond the instrumentalism of settlement services toward seeing settlement services as a pedagogical space of learning and connecting.

Recognizing the life and death realities of refugees who are claiming asylum in another country, Chapter 3 by Susan M. Brigham, Catherine Baillie Abidi, Evangelia Tastsoglou, and Elizabeth Lange examines the informal learning and emotion work of service providers who accompany refugee claimants through the refugee application process. The authors describe the changing international context since 9/11, as nations have heightened security policies that work against humanitarian provisions for, and vulnerabilities of, refugees. This chapter reviews new empirical research that highlights the informal workplace learning needed by service providers to navigate changing policies and service provisions. It also details the toll that emotion work takes on frontline workers who assist refugee claimants and ways adult educators can help build the capacity of service providers and a positive climate for refugees.

In Chapter 4, Yan Guo examines English as a Second Language (ESL) programs in relation to enhancing the employability of immigrants, citizenship participation, and social integration. She begins with an overview of language education in relation to policy and explicates the Canadian policies of bilingualism and multiculturalism, their exclusionary impacts, and the shift from assimilation to employability in ESL programming. Finally, she describes the objective of integration, as a two-way process between newcomers and Canadian-born people, and deconstructs ESL practices that still foster assimilation, White/Christian/middle class "Canadian" values, English linguistic and Anglo cultural norms, and "ideal" workers for the labor market. She challenges adult educators to examine any deficit perspectives they may carry and to become cultural brokers.

In Chapter 5, Tara Gibb examines the context of a global knowledge economy that demands sophisticated use of language and text. Measurement tools have now become standard practice and the expansion of international assessments illustrates how language and literacy are tied to border gatekeeping and labor regulation. Modernist understandings of language as fixed systems are being challenged by approaches like New Literacy Studies that understand language as complex social practices that are situational, sociocultural, and political. Gibb reviews various tests, frameworks, and programs, critiquing the narrow understanding of labor markets toward language ability, the deficit approach to language and literacy, and increased accountability cultures. Finally, she makes the argument that plural ways of knowing and knowledge systems are advantageous, not deficits, and are important for practices of social inclusion.

Bonnie L. Slade, in Chapter 6, describes the flow of professional knowledge across national borders and the multiple systems of professional regulation, higher education, and workplace learning encountered by immigrants. Attracting highly educated professionals has become a key immigration policy in many Western nations based on the assumption that professionals will be able to practice their profession. Research illustrates that this is not the case, partially due to lack of recognition for credentials or prior learning and experience, resulting in immigrant professionals, particularly women, becoming deskilled into low-end jobs, underemployed, or excluded from the labor market. Too often, adult education is implicated in deskilling and exploitation through unnecessary retraining and volunteer programs in professionally unrelated fields.

In Chapter 7, Edward Joaquin and Juanita Johnson-Bailey address the larger structural realities in immigration dynamics. Using a postcolonial perspective, they examine the story of immigration in the United States through race and gender, as interlocking systems of oppression. They unpack the "kinder and hypothetically gentler" forms of racism and discrimination that work to protect the privileges of the dominant ethnoracial group. Gendered practices, such as preventing the immigration of Asian women, the sexual exploitation of women of color, and the feminization of immigration, are also discussed. They conclude by advocating for high-quality transnational education of adults as necessary for social inclusion.

Chapter 8 by Mary V. Alfred explores a new field of inquiry called Diaspora Studies, including historical and contemporary concepts of diaspora, various forms of diaspora, and the heterogeneity of diasporic communities. Alfred advances an agenda for the development of global citizenship adult education, which critically analyzes assumptions about globalization and citizenship as well as hegemonic forms of identity and place that inform citizenship. She advocates for bottom-up globalization that is ecological and people centered and recognizes marginalized forms of knowing, identity, and belonging.

Chapter 9 by Elizabeth Lange and Catherine Baillie Abidi concludes the collection, synthesizing key themes and reflecting on challenges for adult educators. Themes include the three waves of migration, the dominance of national self-interest, historical trends of assimilation, current trends of transnational migration and transborder injustice, and increasingly difficult and exclusionary realities for migrants. Using Nancy Fraser's framework of redistributive, recognitive, and representational justice, the chapter ends with a synthesis of the recommendations for innovations in settlement practices and adult education programs, seeing them both as pedagogical spaces for building welcoming, inclusive communities.

Shibao Guo
Elizabeth Lange
Editors

References

Fraser, N. (2009). *Scales of justice*. New York, NY: Columbia University Press.
Organisation for Economic Co-operation and Development (OECD). (2013). *International migration outlook 2013*. Paris: OECD Publishing. doi:10.1787/migr_outlook-2013-en

SHIBAO GUO *is an associate professor in adult learning at the University of Calgary and currently serves as the president of the Canadian Ethnic Studies Association and as a coeditor of* Canadian Ethnic Studies.

ELIZABETH LANGE *is an associate professor in the Department of Adult Education at St. Francis Xavier University, Canada, and is also an associate editor for the* Canadian Journal for the Study of Adult Education.

This chapter examines the changing nature of adult education in the age of transnational migration and proposes recognitive adult education as an inclusive model that acknowledges and affirms cultural difference and diversity as positive and desirable assets.

The Changing Nature of Adult Education in the Age of Transnational Migration: Toward a Model of Recognitive Adult Education

Shibao Guo

Migration is a broad term used to describe the movement of populations from one place to another. Often used interchangeably with migration, *immigration* refers to the permanent movement of people from one country to another. Where migration most often refers to the movement of populations between nation–states, *internal migration* is used to describe movements of population within a nation–state. For example, it is claimed that in recent decades China has experienced the largest internal migration in human history. Besides "internal migration" and "international migration," the relatively recent term *transnational migration* describes the multiple and circular migration across transnational spaces of migrants who maintain close contact with their countries of origin. With the development of modern transportation and advanced communication technologies, migration has shifted from *international* to *transnational*, as "multiple, circular and return migrations, rather than a singular great journey from one sedentary space to another, occur across transnational spaces" (Lie, 1995, p. 304). In this view, migrants can no longer be characterized as "uprooted" people who are expected to make a sharp and definitive break from their homelands (Glick Schiller, Basch, & Szanton Blanc, 1995). Instead, their daily lives depend on "multiple and constant interconnections across international borders and whose public identities are configured in relationship to more than one nation-state" (p. 48).

As a result of transnational migration, many countries are becoming increasingly ethnoculturally diverse. As newcomers, adult immigrants need educational programs to help them navigate complex paths to citizenship, and to upgrade their language, knowledge, and skills to fully participate in the host society. As our populations grow more diverse, it is imperative for adult

NEW DIRECTIONS FOR ADULT AND CONTINUING EDUCATION, no. 146, Summer 2015 © 2015 Wiley Periodicals, Inc.
Published online in Wiley Online Library (wileyonlinelibrary.com) • DOI: 10.1002/ace.20127

education to continue its long-standing commitment to social inclusion by working toward a more inclusive adult education squarely focused on the benefit of marginalized adult learners (e.g., workers, farmers, women, racialized minorities). In this regard, it is not clear to what extent adult education has upheld its progressive roots in creating socially just and inclusive education environments for adult immigrants. This chapter examines the changing nature of adult education in the age of transnational migration. The discussion that follows is organized into four parts. It begins with an overview of the contextual information related to transnational migration and moves on to an analysis of theoretical debates. The third part examines the impact of transnational migration on adult education and how adult education has responded. The chapter ends with a discussion of its implications for adult education.

Mapping Transnational Migration

This section maps the landscape of transnational migration, including its scope, magnitude, and trends. Owing to divergence in national contexts as well as differences between and within migrant groups, it is difficult to capture its complexities. Migration takes many forms depending on, among other factors, whether the moving subject is a manual worker, a highly qualified specialist, an entrepreneur, a refugee, or if the impetus for migration is family reunification. The fact that migrants enter their destinations via diverse channels leads us to apply a range of labels to them, e.g., temporary workers, permanent immigrants, or asylum seekers. At present, however, it is not clear exactly how many transnational migrants there are. Global inequality means that transnational migration tends to be from less developed nations to the advanced industrial countries, toward OECD (Organisation for Economic Co-operation and Development) member nations. In order to draw some conclusions on the magnitude of contemporary transnational migration, it is useful to look at the OECD's comprehensive annual report on recent developments in migration in its member countries. According to recent OECD Annual Reports (OECD 2008, 2013), some of the salient features of today's transnational migration trends in OECD countries include the following. First, migration of both permanent and temporary immigrants from outside the OECD to OECD countries continues to increase, from an average of 790,000 persons per year between 1956 and 1976, 1.24 million per year during 1977–1990, and 2.65 million per year from 1991 to 2003. Numbers in 2010 reached almost 4 million. Temporary migration is also increasing but at a slower pace than permanent-type migration, sitting at about 2 million in 2010. Furthermore, asylum seeking in OECD countries rose by more than one fifth in 2011 partially due to the "Arab Spring," exceeding 400,000 for the first time since 2003. On average, immigration accounted for 40% of total population growth over the period 2001–2011 in OECD countries whose populations are still growing.

Second, migrants from Eastern Europe and Asia continue to dominate. In 2011, China (10%), Romania (6%), Poland (5.3%), India (4.7%), the

Philippines (3.1%), and Mexico (3.1%) provided one third of total migrants into OECD countries. Migration to European countries continues to be characterized by free circulation within the European Economic Area (EEA), which rose by 15% in 2011 and is now four times more common relative to migration from elsewhere. Third, the migration of highly skilled workers has increased during the past 2 decades. Many OECD countries have adopted point-based systems for the selection of high-skilled candidates, assigning scores in the areas on their education, skills, and resources. Fourth, depending on the destination country and the period of time considered, 20% to 50% of immigrants leave the host country within 5 years of their arrival, either to return home or to move to a third country (OECD, 2008). Migrants move again for four major reasons, including failure to integrate in the host country, individuals' desire to return to their home countries, achievement of a savings objective, or the opening of employment opportunities in their home countries (OECD, 2008). The 2013 report indicates that flows out of southern European countries most affected by the economic crisis (e.g., Greece, Italy, Portugal, Spain) accelerated by 45% from 2009 to 2011 (OECD, 2013). Many countries continue to seek ways of encouraging skilled members of these diaspora to return.

As a result of transnational migration, the foreign-born population of OECD countries as a whole reached 12.5% of the total population in 2011, representing an increase by about 30 million persons over 10 years (2001–2011). Among the top immigrant-receiving countries, 26.8% of Australia's citizens were foreign born, followed by Canada at 20.6%, Germany at 13%, the United States at 12.9%, and the United Kingdom at 11.5% (OECD, 2013). It is predicted that the populations of other OECD member states will increasingly resemble these countries in the coming years with respect to both prevalence and diversity.

Theorizing Transnational Migration

In articulating transnational migration, Lie (1995) argues that "the idea of transnationalism challenges the rigid, territorial nationalism that defines the modern nation-state" (p. 304). According to Lie, "transnationalism" makes it possible for imagined diaspora communities to subvert old conceptions of unidirectional migrant passage and replace them with understandings centered on images of unending sojourn across different lands. It seems clear that the concept of transnationalism provides the necessary theoretical underpinning for transnational migration, which is the focus of this section.

Transnationalism is not a new concept per se. According to Kivisto (2001), the earliest articulation of transnationalism was by cultural anthropologists (i.e., Nina Glick Schiller, Linda Basch, and Christina Szanton Blanc). In its debut in the early 1990s it offered a novel analytical approach to understanding contemporary migration. Sociologist Alejandro Portes is most responsible for popularizing and expanding the use of transnationalism (Portes, 1999, 2003; Portes, Guarnizo, & Landolt, 1999). Portes et al. (1999) propose three criteria for identifying a transnational phenomenon: the process involves a significant proportion of persons in the relevant universe; the activities of interest possess certain stability and resilience over time; and the content of these activities is not captured by some preexisting concept. When analyzing transnationalism, individuals and their support networks are regarded as the proper units of analysis. According to Portes et al., a study that begins with the history and activities of individuals is "the most efficient way of learning about the institutional underpinnings of transnationalism and its structural effects" (p. 220). Unlike early transnationalism, which was often limited to elites, contemporary grassroots transnational activities have developed in reaction to government policies—and to the condition of dependent capitalism foisted on weaker countries—to circumvent the permanent subordination of immigrants and their families. At the grassroots level, Portes (1999) points out elsewhere, transnationalism offers an economic alternative to immigrants' low-wage dead-end employment situation, gives them political voice, and allows them to reaffirm their own self-worth.

Transitional activities can be organized into three types: economic, political, and sociocultural (Portes et al., 1999). The main goals of each type are different. To be more specific, transnational economic entrepreneurs are interested in mobilizing their contacts across borders in search of suppliers, capital, and markets; transnational political activities aim to foster political power and influence in sending or receiving countries; and sociocultural transnationalism is oriented toward the reinforcement of a national identity abroad or the collective enjoyment of cultural events and goods. Another useful distinction is made between transnationalism "from above" and "from below," initiated respectively by powerful states and corporations, and by grassroots immigrants and their home country counterparts. In commenting on the fear that transnational activities will slow down the process of assimilation in immigrant host nations, Portes (1999) maintains that transnational activities can actually facilitate successful adaptation by providing opportunities for economic mobility and for a vital and purposeful group life. He also points out that the overall bearing of transnational activities on sending countries is positive, both economically and politically. Migrant remittances and business investments promote economic growth, and political activism is most likely to align with the forces of change in promoting democracy and reducing corruption and violation of human rights at home. Portes (2003) further argues that transnationalism provides "an alternative path of socioeconomic and political adaptation to the host society not envisioned by traditional models of assimilation" (p. 887).

Researching Transnational Migration and Adult Education

Despite the long tradition of adult education in serving marginalized groups, until recently there has been a lack of interest among adult educators in issues related to transnational migration (Alfred & Guo, 2012). Transnational migration did not draw the attention of the international adult education community until the new millennium when Canadian scholars (Mojab, Ng, & Mirchandani, 2000) organized the first roundtable focused on the concept at the joint AERC (Adult Education Research Conference) and CASAE (Canadian Association for the Study of Adult Education) conference in Vancouver. Since then we have witnessed an emerging critical scholarship in studies related to transnational migration and adult education focusing on the following topics: devaluation of immigrants' prior learning and work experience, marginalization of immigrant women, volunteering and informal learning, and community-based adult education.

Devaluation of Immigrants' Foreign Credentials. Deskilling and devaluation of immigrants' prior learning and work experience is one of most important issues studied by international adult educators. Despite many countries' preference for highly skilled immigrants and the fact that immigrants bring significant human capital resources to the host country, many well-educated immigrants encounter difficulties in integrating into the host society due to a lack of recognition of prior learning and work experience (Andersson & Fejes, 2010; Brandi, 2001; Guo, 2009, 2013; Morrice, 2013; Shan, 2009a, 2009b; Wagner & Childs, 2006). In Australia, where recruitment addresses specific skills gaps and labor market shortages, skilled migrants, particularly those from culturally and linguistically diverse backgrounds, face an ironic situation. Those whose skills are most needed encounter special difficulties in gaining access to these professions (Wagner & Childs, 2006). As Wagner and Childs observe, immigrant optometrists become taxi drivers, social workers become hospital cleaners, teachers become clerical assistants, and environmental engineers stack supermarket shelves. Unfortunately, this experience is not unique to Australia. Italy's "brain gain" has become a "brain waste" (Brandi, 2001). Brandi reports that more than 40% of Rome's skilled migrants, particularly these from Africa, Asia, and Latin America, work in low-skill jobs. Immigrants in Canada face similar challenges. Guo (2013) uses the triple glass effect to illustrate the multiple layers of structural barriers facing immigrant professionals in Canada as a result of devaluation of their prior learning and work experiences, including *a glass gate*, *a glass door*, and *a glass ceiling*. A *glass gate* denies immigrants' entrance to guarded professional communities, and *a glass door* blocks immigrants' access to professional employment at high-wage firms. Finally, *a glass ceiling* prevents immigrants from moving into management positions because of their ethnic and cultural differences. Highly educated refugees in Sweden and the United Kingdom encounter similar barriers (Andersson & Fejes, 2010; Morrice, 2013).

Lack of access to the professional occupations for which immigrants have prior learning and work experience leads to unemployment and underemployment, poor economic performance, and downward social mobility. In tracing its root causes, Guo (2009) attributed the devaluation phenomenon to epistemological misperceptions of difference and knowledge and an objectivist ontology and liberal universalism. The deficit model of difference leads to conflation of "difference" and "deficiency," as well as a belief that the knowledge of immigrant professionals, particularly those from developing countries, is incompatible and inferior, and, hence, invalid. Knowledge has been racialized and materialized on the basis of ethnic and national origin. Furthermore, our commitment to an objectivist ontology and liberal universalism exacerbates the complexity of this process. Guo's study demonstrates that by applying a one-size-fits-all criterion to the measurement of immigrants' credentials and experience, liberal universalism denies immigrants opportunities to be successful in the new society. It also reveals that discourses of "professional standards" and "excellence" have been used as a cloak to restrict competition and legitimize existing power relations. Once heralded by adult educators as potentially the most radical innovation since the introduction of mass formal education, it seems evident that prior learning assessment and recognition (PLAR) has become a serious barrier to adult learning rather than a facilitator. The difficulties immigrant professionals face in being recognized in the host society suggest that PLAR procedures have been deployed as technologies of power and a system of governing in discounting and devaluating immigrants' prior learning and work experience, thus reducing adult education to a system of exclusion and a mode of social control (Andersson & Guo, 2009).

Marginalization of Immigrant Women. The situation of immigrant women is worse still. A number of studies demonstrate that immigrant women face multiple barriers in adapting to the host society, particularly in accessing the labor market, owing to disadvantages attributed to gender, class, and race (Gibb & Hamdon, 2010; Maitra & Shan, 2007; Mojab, 1999; Ng, 1999; Shan, 2009a, 2009b). Feminist scholars argue that, in the labor force, the category of "immigrant women" serves to commodify these women to employers (Mojab, 1999; Ng, 1999). Their existing lower class positions are reinforced when they provide cheap, docile labor to the state under exploitive conditions, often permeated with racism and sexism. Maitra and Shan (2007) showed how highly skilled professional immigrant women learn to reorient and reshape their skills, experiences, and aspirations in order to secure employment in ways that can be both conformative and transgressive. In a study with immigrant women in Toronto, Shan (2009b) found that the women resort to retraining and reeducation as a means to improve their employment prospects. She uses the credential and certificate regime to explain the social process and practices that attribute differential values to credentials and certificates produced in different places. Some women also resort to strategic tolerance, mobilize their prior knowledge and expertise, and become agents of change (Shan, 2009a). Shan further argues that the legitimate space presupposed in situated learning was an entitlement that the women had to earn in Canada. Crucially, adult educators took up these issues and examined how gender, class, and race interacted to shape the experience of immigrant women, particularly women of color.

Volunteering and Informal Learning. Volunteering has been identified by many researchers as a powerful source of informal learning (Guo, 2014; Sawchuk, 2008; Slade & Schugurensky, 2010). Immigrants volunteer for a range of reasons, from altruism to learning new skills for career advancement. Through volunteering, immigrants learn the necessary language, skills, and knowledge required of new citizens for successful integration into the host society. Immigrants consider informal learning from the volunteer experience to be more significant than formal, job-related training. One of the most valued areas of learning through this process is communication skills. As alluded to earlier, one of the most prominent issues facing immigrants is unemployment and underemployment. In this context, volunteering has been adopted by many immigrants as a strategy to gain local work experience and improve their access to the labor market (Slade & Schugurensky, 2010). Volunteering and informal learning are seen as important stepping stones for the integration of immigrants in helping them navigate the complex paths to citizenship. Unlike traditional forms of volunteering, which are freely chosen, the decision of immigrants to volunteer is often the result of labor market pressures. In this sense, Slade and Schugurensky (2010) argue, for immigrants volunteering is more coerced than an expression of individual freedom. Furthermore, volunteering helps immigrants build a community and a sense of belonging. Immigrants participate in volunteer activities to fulfill their social responsibilities as active citizens to take collective action in providing mutual support to newcomers, helping them overcome barriers in settlement and adaptation in the new society (Guo, 2014). In this sense, volunteering becomes an important site for the kind of social action and emancipatory learning that Foley (1999) speaks of.

Community-Based Adult Education. A number of studies investigate the potential for community organizations to act as spaces and places of adult education for recent immigrants (Guo, 2006; Guo & Guo, 2011; Jackson, 2010; Kim, 2010). A common issue faced in serving immigrants lies in the "sameness" approach, which treats all adult learners as having the same learning needs and backgrounds, thus negating and denigrating immigrant learners' rich sociocultural diversity and complexity (Guo, 2010). As a consequence, many adult immigrant learners feel alienated and excluded. Because mainstream adult education organizations fail to provide immigrants with education programs that are culturally and linguistically accessible and appropriate, community-based adult education has become an alternative in providing inclusive and equitable programs to adult immigrants. In Canada, ethnocultural organizations play an important role in promoting adult and lifelong education (Guo, 2006; Guo & Guo, 2011). They are effective and responsive in providing culturally and linguistically accessible and appropriate educational programs to adult immigrants, including language education, employment programs, business development and training, counseling services, and community development. Their programs have helped immigrants ease the process of settlement and adaptation. More important, they have created homes and communities to which immigrants feel they belong. Elsewhere, Jackson (2010) in the United Kingdom and Kim (2010) in South Korea report similar findings. In particular, they emphasize the importance of the social spaces these organizations have created, which enable immigrants to network with each other to affirm identities and develop relational capital and an enhanced sense of belonging. As transitional institutions, they have acted as stepping stones for immigrants to integrate into mainstream society and as mediators between individual immigrant and receiving states. They also demonstrate that communities are important sites for emancipatory learning and social action (Cunningham, 2000).

Conclusion: Toward a Model of Recognitive Adult Education

The discussion in this chapter highlights the changing landscape of adult education characterized by cross-disciplinary and multidisciplinary orientations and activities focusing on the complexity of immigrant experiences. The four themes that emerge from this analysis demonstrate that the changing diversity resulting from transnational migration poses both challenges and new opportunities for further development in adult education. In the process of building inclusive adult education, we have witnessed two prominent challenges confronting adult educators in our daily practice: the "difference as deficit" perspective, which views difference as deficiency, and the "sameness" approach, which assumes that all learners have the same background and learning needs. Despite adult education's long-standing commitment to social justice, this analysis demonstrates that the field has played a dual role in responding to transnational migration and cultural diversity as both enabler and constrainer. Immigrant women's marginalized experiences and the devaluation of immigrants' prior learning and work experience suggest that adult education has created a system of exclusion and a model of social control. In this sense, adult education has failed to respond positively to the changing needs of adult immigrants and failed to embrace cultural diversity and difference that recent immigrant learners bring to adult education settings. On the other hand, community-based, informal learning indicates that adult education has created important spaces for emancipatory learning and social action. In this view, adult education remains an enabler.

To reclaim the radical roots of adult education for social inclusion, I propose *recognitive adult education* as a paradigm shift in building inclusive and socially just educational environments. Recognitive adult education is in alignment with the principles of recognitive justice, which provide an expanded understanding of social justice insisting that we must not only rethink what we mean by social justice but also acknowledge the place of social and cultural groups within this space (Fraser, 2000, 2008, 2009; Gale & Densmore, 2000; Guo, 2010). Recognitive justice advocates three necessary conditions for social justice: the fostering of respect for different social groups through their self-identification, opportunities for self-development and self-expression, and the participation of groups in decision making through group representation (Gale & Densmore, 2000). Because a society without intragroup differences is neither possible nor desirable, recognizing the validity of social and cultural groups is essential for their identity, sense of worth, and self-esteem (Fraser, 2000, 2008, 2009; Honneth, 2008). Fraser explains that claims for recognition have become the "paradigmatic form of political conflict" since the late 20th century (Fraser, 2008, p. 188). Treating recognition as a matter of social status, she argues that the struggle for recognition means "examining institutionalized patterns of cultural value for the effects on the relative standing of social actors" (Fraser, 2000, p. 113). To be misrecognised, according to Fraser, is to be denied the status of a full partner in social interaction, which constitutes a form of institutionalized subordination and a serious violation of justice. In this view, redressing misrecognition should aim at overcoming subordination, replacing institutionalized value patterns that impede parity of participation with ones that foster it. To achieve this goal, Fraser suggests developing a critical theory of recognition that can coherently combine two analytically distinct kinds of remedy, redistribution and recognition, which are fundamental to achieving the justice of representation that ensures equal political voice (Fraser, 2009).

This notion of recognitive justice informs the notion of recognitive adult education, offering a broadened perspective on migration that recognizes its transnational flows and concomitant diasporic allegiances and affiliations. It seeks to balance freedom of mobility with protection, recognition, and membership. Recognitive adult education rejects the deficit model of adult education that seeks to assimilate migrants to the dominant social, cultural, and educational norms of the host society. It proposes instead to build an inclusive education that acknowledges and affirms cultural difference and diversity as positive and desirable assets. These assets are seen as a means of ensuring the participation of individuals from socially and culturally differentiated groups in social, political, and educational institutions. It challenges Eurocentric perspectives, standards, and values and accepts currently marginalized knowledges as valid and valuable expressions of the human experience. This framework will inform policymakers, researchers, and practitioners in developing inclusive policies and initiatives in the area of adult education, immigrant settlement and integration, work, and learning in order to embrace people from different ethnic and cultural backgrounds.

References

Alfred, M. V., & Guo, S. (2012). Toward global citizenship: Internationalization of adult education in Canada and the US. *Canadian Journal for the Study of Adult Education*, 24(2), 51–69.

Andersson, P., & Fejes, A. (2010). Mobility of knowledge as a recognition challenge: Experiences from Sweden. *International Journal of Lifelong Education*, 29(2), 201–218.

Andersson, P., & Guo, S. (2009). Governing through non/recognition: The missing "R" in the PLAR for immigrant professionals in Canada and Sweden. *International Journal of Lifelong Education*, 28(4), 423–437.

Brandi, M. C. (2001). Skilled immigrants in Rome. *International Migration*, 39(4), 101–116.

Cunningham, P. (2000). The sociology of adult education. In A. Wilson & E. Hayes (Eds.), *Handbook of adult and continuing education* (pp. 573–591). San Francisco, CA: Jossey-Bass.

Foley, G. (1999). *Learning in social action: A contribution to understanding informal education*. London, UK: Zed Books.

Fraser, N. (2000). Rethinking recognition. *New Left Review, 3*, 107–120.

Fraser, N. (2008). From redistribution to recognition? Dilemmas of justice in "postsocialist" age. In S. Seidman & J. Alexander (Eds.), *The new social theory reader* (pp. 188–196). London, UK: Routledge.

Fraser, N. (2009). *Scales of justice: Reimagining political space in a globalizing world*. New York, NY: Columbia University Press.

Gale, T., & Densmore, K. (2000). *Just schooling: Explorations in the cultural politics of teaching*. Buckingham, UK: Open University Press.

Gibb, T., & Hamdon, E. (2010). Moving across borders: Immigrant women's encounters with globalization, the knowledge economy and lifelong learning. *International Journal of Lifelong Education, 29*(2), 185–200.

Glick Schiller, N., Basch, L., & Szanton Blanc, C. (1995). From immigrant to transmigrant: Theorizing transnational migration. *Anthropological Quarterly, 68*(1), 48–63.

Guo, S. (2006). Adult education for social change: The role of a grassroots organization in Canada. *Convergence, 39*(4), 107–122.

Guo, S. (2009). Difference, deficiency, and devaluation: Tracing the roots of non/recognition of foreign credentials for immigrant professionals in Canada. *Canadian Journal for the Study of Adult Education, 22*(1), 37–52.

Guo, S. (2010). Toward recognitive justice: Emerging trends and challenges in transnational migration and lifelong learning. *International Journal of Lifelong Education, 29*(2), 149–167.

Guo, S. (2013). Economic integration of recent Chinese immigrants in Canada's second-tier cities: The triple glass effect and immigrants' downward social mobility. *Canadian Ethnic Studies, 45*(3), 95–115.

Guo, S. (2014). Immigrants as active citizens: Exploring the volunteering experience of Chinese immigrants in Vancouver. *Globalisation, Societies and Education, 12*(1), 51–70.

Guo, S., & Guo, Y. (2011). Multiculturalism, ethnicity and minority rights: The complexity and paradox of ethnic organizations in Canada. *Canadian Ethnic Studies, 43*(1–2), 59–80.

Honneth, A. (2008). Personal identity and disrespect. In S. Seidman and J. Alexander (Eds.), *The new social theory reader* (pp. 43–49). London, UK: Routledge.

Jackson, S. (2010). Learning through social spaces: Migrant women and lifelong learning in post-colonial London. *International Journal of Lifelong Education, 29*(2), 237–253.

Kim, J. H. (2010). A changed context of lifelong learning under the influence of migration: South Korea. *International Journal of Lifelong Education, 29*(2), 255–272.

Kivisto, P. (2001). Theorizing transnational immigration: A critical review of current efforts. *Ethnic and Racial Studies, 24*(4), 549–577.

Lie, J. (1995). From international migration to transnational diaspora. *Contemporary Sociology, 24*(4), 303–306.

Maitra, S., & Shan, H. (2007). Transgressive vs conformative: Immigrant women learning at contingent work. *Journal of Workplace Learning, 19*(5), 286–295.

Mojab, S. (1999). De-skilling immigrant women. *Canadian Woman Studies, 19*(3), 123–128.

Mojab, S., Ng, R., & Mirchandani, K. (2000). Immigrant women and labour flexibility: Resisting training through learning. In *Proceedings of the AERC and CASAE joint conference*. Vancouver, BC: University of British Columbia.

Morrice, L. (2013). Refugees in higher education: Boundaries of belonging and recognition, stigma and exclusion. *International Journal of Lifelong Education, 32*(5), 652–668.

Ng, R. (1999). Homeworking: Dream realized or freedom constrained? The globalized reality of immigrant garment workers. *Canadian Woman Studies, 19*(3), 110–114.

OECD. (2008). *International migration outlook*. Paris, France: Organisation for Economic Co-operation and Development.

OECD. (2013). *International migration outlook*. Paris, France: Organisation for Economic Co-operation and Development.

Portes, A. (1999). Conclusion: Towards a new world—the origin and effects of transnational activities. *Ethnic and Racial Studies, 22*(2), 463–477.

Portes, A. (2003). Conclusion: Theoretical convergencies and empirical evidence in the study of immigrant transnationalism. *International Migration Review, 37*(3), 874–892.

Portes, A., Guarnizo, L. E., & Landolt, P. (1999). The study of transnationalism: Pitfalls and promise of an emergent research field. *Ethnic and Racial Studies, 22*(2), 217–237.

Sawchuk, P. H. (2008). Theories and methods for research on informal learning and work: Towards cross-fertilization. *Studies in Continuing Education, 30*(1), 1–16.

Shan, H. (2009a). Practices on the periphery: Highly educated Chinese immigrant women negotiating occupational settlement in Canada. *Canadian Journal for the Study of Adult Education, 21*(2), 1–18.

Shan, H. (2009b). Shaping the re-training and re-education experiences of immigrant women: The credential and certificate regime in Canada. *International Journal of Lifelong Education, 28*(3), 353–369.

Slade, B., & Schugurensky, D. (2010). "Starting from another side, the bottom": Volunteer work as a transition into the labour market for immigrant professionals. In P. Sawchuk and A. Taylor (Eds.), *Challenging transitions in learning and work: Perspectives on policy and practice* (pp. 261–281). Rotterdam, the Netherlands: Sense Publishers.

Wagner, R., & Childs, M. (2006). Exclusionary narratives as barriers to the recognition of qualifications, skills and experience—a case of skilled migrants in Australia. *Studies in Continuing Education, 28*(1), 49–62.

SHIBAO GUO is an associate professor in adult learning at the University of Calgary and currently serves as the president of the Canadian Ethnic Studies Association and as a coeditor of Canadian Ethnic Studies.

2

This chapter focuses on the shifting roles that settlement services play in immigrant training and education and advocates a mode of participatory governance.

Settlement Services in the Training and Education of Immigrants: Toward a Participatory Mode of Governance

Hongxia Shan

Settler countries such as Canada, New Zealand, and Australia have had a history of providing formal and informal services to immigrants and refugees, often during their initial period of settlement. This chapter provides a historical review of the policies, practices, and research related to settlement or immigrant services in Canada, with particular attention paid to the roles that they have played in immigrant training and education vis-à-vis labor market segmentation and deprofessionalization. It also identifies the ideological shifts underlying settlement services and highlights what I call a participatory mode of governance as an alternative way to reimagine training and services for immigrants.

A Historical Overview of Immigrant Services in Canada

Prior to World War II, immigrant settlement was primarily the responsibility of immigrants themselves and those who brought them to Canada. Companies such as the Canadian National Railway, Canadian Pacific Railway, and Hudson Bay, family members already settled in Canada, ethnic communities and organizations, churches, and settlement houses were the major players in immigrants' settlement (Amin, 1987; Integration Branch, 2001). Additionally, educational institutions were involved in inducting and assimilating migrant workers to the host society and labor market. For instance, as early as the 1890s, Alfred Fitzpatrick, the founder of Frontier College, and his colleagues went from camp to camp to deliver basic literacy programs to young lumber workers, many of whom were immigrants.

The Canadian state was not involved in immigrant services until 1948. At that time, settlement services were mainly set up to assist families of Canadian soldiers and war refugees to adjust to life in Canada. In 1966, when the

New Directions for Adult and Continuing Education, no. 146, Summer 2015 © 2015 Wiley Periodicals, Inc.
Published online in Wiley Online Library (wileyonlinelibrary.com) • DOI: 10.1002/ace.20128

19

new Department of Manpower and Immigration (renamed Citizenship and Immigration Canada in 1993) was created, the state discontinued settlement services. The prevailing philosophy was that immigrants should turn to existing mainstream services available to all Canadians. The retrenchment of settlement services could not have happened at a worse time, especially in view of the changing demography of immigrants and the systematic barriers newcomers faced integrating into the host labor market.

The changing demography of immigrants had to do with the shift of immigration policies in the 1960s. Until the late 1960s, immigration policies in Canada were overtly racialized, biased against people of color. Given the dwindling supply of immigrants from European countries, the Canadian Government then introduced the point system, which admits immigrants based on their educational and work experiences rather than their countries of origin. As a result of this policy shift, immigrants started coming in large numbers from Asia, Africa, and Latin America. Accompanying the change to the racial composition of immigrants has been the changing economic outcomes of newcomers. Despite their educational backgrounds, new immigrants, especially those from nontraditional immigrant source countries, find it hard to get their qualifications recognized in Canada. As a result, they are often underemployed, deprofessionalized, or employed at the margins of a labor market segmented along relations of difference, such as race and gender (e.g., Tastsoglou & Preston, 2005).

The changing demography of immigrants nevertheless posed challenges to the national identity of Canada as a settlement country of the British and French on Indigenous lands. As the immigration policies changed, not only was the demand for equal status heightened within the French community, but other ethnic groups also called on the government to recognize their contributions to Canadian society. In response, the Canadian Government announced the policy of multiculturalism in 1971 (Esses & Gardner, 1996). Subsequently in 1974, the Department of Manpower and Immigration expanded its mandate and assumed responsibility for coordinating immigrant services. In particular, it established the Immigrant Settlement and Adaptation Program, which has since provided funding to nongovernmental organizations to deliver settlement services such as information, orientation, and referral to services. Today, in addition to the federal government, provincial and other local governments, charitable organizations and private foundations also provide funding for immigrant services. Delivery of services is often conducted through nongovernmental organizations, particularly community-based organizations, including ethnic-specific immigrant service agencies (Omidvar & Richmond, 2003), as well as educational institutions (e.g., Friesen, 2011; Slade, 2012).

From Assimilation to Integration

A closer review of the history of immigrant services in Canada also shows a discursive and ideological shift from assimilation to integration. In her preliminary overview of settlement work in the province of Ontario, Amin (1987) pointed out that prior to 1949 informal settlement services were often conducted out of a framework of paternalism and the call for "Christian duty" to Canadianize the "coarse," "uncivilized," and "unsanitized" immigrants. Other historical documents also show that settlement workers, trainers, and educators often took upon themselves the task of Canadianizing the "unlearned" immigrants. For example, in his *Handbook for New Canadians*, Alfred Fitzpatrick, founder of the Frontier Institute, wrote:

> We allow new-comers to live in settlements on the prairies or, what is worse, to form colonies in large urban and industrial cent[er]s. There, their racial char-acteristics are continued and encouraged by native societies and leagues, form-ing unassimilated groups, which are a menace to Canadian unity. Already there are whole sections of alien races in Montreal, Toronto, Hamilton, Winnipeg, Vancouver, and other cent[er]s. The tendency is for the foreign-born to make little effort for naturali[zation]. We have a right to demand that every man who comes to Canada become a citizen of this country. Unlearned masses of non-English-speaking races are fertile soil for future trouble. ... Both the immigrant by means of night classes, and the immigrants' children in the day schools, must learn to take a pride in the land they have chosen, by making them acquainted with the language, customs, and laws of their new home country. (Fitzpatrick, 1919, pp. 1–2)

Clearly, not only were immigrants expected to assimilate, but ethnic commu-nities and organizations were also considered a barrier to immigrants' assim-ilative processes.

In the wake of World War II, Canada experienced mass migration mainly from war-torn countries in Europe. Subsequently, religious, volunteer, and ethnic organizations enhanced their settlement support for immigrants. The notion of integration also emerged during this time, initially in the article, "Postwar Integration of Immigrants" in the *1959 Canada Year Book* (Tolley & Young, 2011). The ideal of integration was then reiterated in the series of mul-ticulturalism acts introduced by the government. Today, integration stands as a core of Canadian immigration policy, i.e., the 2001 Immigration and Refugee Protection Act. The act states that one of the objectives of immigration is "to promote the successful integration of residents into Canada while recognizing that integration involves mutual obligations for new immigrants and Canadian society" (CIC, 2001, p. 1).

The shift from an assimilative to an integrative approach has not been particular to Canada. New Zealand and Australia, two other countries founded through the settlement of immigrants, also went through similar transitions as Canada at around the same time. Despite the converging policy shift to integra-tion, settlement services in these countries vary in many ways. New Zealand, for instance, offers only initial services through a limited number of govern-ment agencies (CIC, 2011). Australia, which has similar levels of immigration as Canada and adopted an immigration policy similar to Canada's point system, has experimented with different settlement policies and programs. Over the past decade, the Australia government has moved its settlement services from a free welfare model to a user pay model. For instance, should skilled immigrants need English training for vocational purposes, they can access related training services but on a loan basis. Once employed, they have to return a percentage of the cost of the program through additional taxation (CIC, 2011). In light of the retraction of services in other countries, Canada's settlement services have been upheld as exemplary. This is not only because immigrant services in Canada are typically free of charge to immigrants but also because of the involvement of community-based organizations and other stakeholders in the delivery of related services (CIC, 2011; Richmond & Shields, 2005). What distinguishes Canadian settlement services is also the emergence of what I call a participatory mode of governance in the imagination, conceptualization, and management of settlement services.

Toward a Participatory Mode of Governance

Although integration has officially been made a goal for immigration and settlement in Canada, how to integrate this ideal into practice remains a challenge. There are, however, important movements on the ground and emerging institutional spaces that adumbrate a participatory mode of governance, which involves immigrants in the design and delivery of the services. I argue that this is the most promising approach for best practice in settlement services. As illustrated previously, community-based organizations historically have been an important player in settling immigrants in Canada. Some community activists have proposed a bold vision to reimagine settlement services. For instance, Ratna Omidvar, a first-generation immigrant and the executive director of the Maytree Foundation, a private foundation that promotes equity and diversity and helps immigrants to settle, called on immigrants to be participatory actors in the making of settlement policies and practices (Omidvar, 2001). Specifically, she proposed that first a national coalition of immigrants and interested individuals be established to inform the public and the governments on immigration and settlement policies. Second, she encouraged immigrants to participate in local community affairs. Third, she argued that cities should take on a more central leadership role in integrating immigrants, as they are closer to the realities of immigrants' lives than the provincial and federal governments. Finally, she suggested that professional organizations of settlement workers need to not only serve the profession but also enter formally into the field as policy actors (Omidvar, 2001).

What I refer to as a participatory mode of governance can also be traced to *Best Settlement Practices* and the *Canadian National Settlement Service Standards Framework*, two policy documents developed in 1998 and 2000 by the Canadian Council for Refugees, a national nonprofit umbrella organization committed in part to the settlement of refugees and immigrants in Canada.

Both documents were created as part of the federal government's consultation process on settlement renewal that started in 1995. Both emphasize core values such as access, inclusion, client empowerment, holistic approaches, user-defined services, cultural sensitivity, community development, collaboration, and accountability (Canadian Council for Refugees, 1998, 2000). Among these values, client empowerment, holistic approaches, and collaboration in particular open up spaces for participatory governance. For instance, to assure client empowerment, the following best-practice guidelines were proposed:

> Fostering independence in clients; meaningful membership and participation of clients in the Board; encouraging client involvement in all areas of the organization; involving clients as volunteers; recognizing, affirming and building on the resources, experiences, skills and wisdom of newcomers; providing information and education to allow clients to make their own informed decisions; offering programs and services leading to employment and career advancement; offering supportive environment (especially to those who are traumatized); supporting the clients right to choose from among service providers the approach that best meets their needs. (Canadian Council for Refugees, 2000, "Core Values")

Whereas the emphasis on independence strongly resonates with the desire of the Canadian state for immigrants to be economically productive upon landing (Sedef, 1999), these guidelines allow for and indeed encourage immigrants to participate in the conceptualization, management, and delivery of settlement services. Specifically, immigrants are encouraged to be involved in boards of governance and other service organization activities. More important, these guidelines uphold a strengths-based approach; instead of asking immigrants to become us, they emphasize "recognizing, affirming and building on the resources, experiences, skills and wisdom of newcomers" (Canadian Council for Refugees, 2000, "Core Values").

Although there is little documentation on how individual immigrants have participated in the management of immigrant services, historically, places have been made within the institution of settlement services where ethnic organizations exert influence on the kind of services that are provided. In *Immigrant Settlement Policy in Canadian Municipalities*, Tolley and Young (2011) examined settlement policies and practices in a number of municipalities in Canada. They showed that although governments of different levels have proven to be significant in shaping immigrant services from the top down through funding and accountability mechanisms, there are also influential bottom-up social forces. Andrew and Hima (2011), for instance, understood settlement services as an example of a mixed mode of government and governance; the government dimension involves horizontal and vertical coordination within and between federal, provincial, and municipal governments, whereas the governance dimension involves nonstate actors, such as ethnic minority organizations. In their case study, they found that the federal government's interest in supporting the development of official-language minority communities was the result of growing activity of the organizations of minority Franco-phone communities. A case study by Stasiulis, Hughes, and Amery (2011), which focused on immigrant settlement policy in Toronto, Ottawa and the Peel, Niagara, and Waterloo regions, also showed the existence of distributed (decentralized) and collaborative modes of governance. These case studies should not be taken to mean that power is equally distributed among the stakeholders. Yet, they clearly show that rather than being the sole purview of the governments, settlement services have been influenced by a range of social forces and stakeholders today.

Toward Best Practices: The Roles of Settlement Services

Currently, Citizenship and Immigration Canada (CIC) is promoting best prac-tices for settlement services online at http://www.cic.gc.ca/english/department/partner/bpss/. Many of the programs it showcases are geared toward immi-grant professionals seeking employment in regulated professional fields. To assess best practices, CIC uses four criteria: accessibility, newcomer involve-ment, stakeholder collaboration, and positive outcomes. To some extent, these criteria reflect the values outlined in *Best Settlement Practices* and *Canadian National Settlement Service Standards Framework* (Canadian Council for Refugees, 1998, 2000), in particular with regard to holistic approach, collaboration, and accountability. However, there is no information as to whether or how the pro-grams have built on immigrants' prior knowledge, resources, and experiences. Furthermore, the majority of the programs showcased seem to have involved immigrants but mostly as recipients of services. What is not known is the ex-tent of involvement of immigrants in the design and management of the pro-grams. To pursue best practices, I believe that it is important to understand the roles that settlement services have played and could play in the training and education of immigrants vis-à-vis labor market segmentation and deprofes-sionalization. In this respect, related research provides much food for thought.

Expanding Cultural Capital Versus Exerting Cultural Imperialism. Often, immigrant services are positioned as instrumental in expanding immi-grants' social and cultural capital and thereby enhancing their opportunities in the host labor market. The success of the programs therefore depends on how well they help immigrants overcome issues of recognition by different stake-holders. For instance, the School of Nursing at York University, with funding from the Ontario Ministry of Citizenship and Immigration, launched a pilot training project in 2007 to advise the nursing regulatory body about candi-dates' professional readiness to write the Canadian Registered Nurse Exami-nation. Although participants learned a great deal through the program, some of them felt misled as there was a lack of recognition of the program by the reg-ulatory body (Van Kleef & Werqin, 2013). In contrast, to address qualification-recognition issues for immigrant engineers newly arrived in Canada, the Engineering Department in the University of Manitoba worked with the regulatory body in the province and developed an Internationally Educated

Engineers Qualification Program. This program has an academic component, a paid work-experience placement with an employer in the participants' engineering discipline, as well as training on Canadian workplace culture (Friesen, 2011). It is believed that the program has been successful exactly because it has expanded immigrants' social and cultural capital, as they are recognized in Canada (Friesen, 2011).

In diametrical contrast to this position, some other researchers suggest that immigrant services mediate an implicit expectation that immigrants need to be instructed to meet the social and cultural standards of the host society. For instance, in her examination of a bridging program for professional immigrants, which was offered through a school board, Slade (2012) found that the program used high-school curriculum for skilled immigrants. She argued that using high-school curriculum for highly skilled immigrants diminishes the skills and knowledge that they bring with them to the host society. If Slade's study suggests cultural condescension in curriculum design, Cervatiuc and Ricento (2012) suggested possible cultural imperialism in pedagogical practices. Through classroom observations and interviews, they found that trainers may take a prescriptive approach to teaching Canadian culture to newcomers, rendering irrelevant immigrants' cultures, epistemological perspectives, and life experiences.

Pseudostate Apparatus Versus a Liminal Space of Change. Just as researchers disagree on the roles that immigrant services play in the domain of culture, they differ in their views on the roles that the services play in the political economy of Canada. Feminist studies of immigrant services suggest that although linking immigrants to the labor market, government-funded programs may also serve an intermediary, if not a pseudostate apparatus, channeling immigrants and immigrant women in particular to gendered and often low-end sectors of the labor market (Mojab, 1999; Ng, 1988). Mojab (1999), for example, attributed this phenomenon to the mixed needs for high-skilled as well as low-skilled labor in the so-called knowledge economy of Canada. Ng (1988) traced the problem to the contractual relationship between service agencies and the government. Funders' demands for accountability, in particular the number of immigrants served, exert pressure on organizations to link immigrant women with "accessible" jobs. In both cases, the social, economic, and cultural location of immigrant women seems to have rendered them particularly susceptible to the pressure to take up any job, regardless of their interest or educational background.

Some studies of immigrants' experiences volunteering in Canada also point to the ambiguous roles that immigrant services may play in entrenching the vulnerability of immigrants in the host labor market. To gain Canadian experiences, immigrants often resort to volunteering (Scott, Selbee, & Reed, 2001) and some immigrant training programs also provide unpaid work placement opportunities for immigrants. Although immigrants may gain valuable learning experiences by volunteering, volunteering is a labor that immigrants contribute to the Canadian labor market without pay (Schugurensky, Slade, &

Luo, 2005; Slade, 2012). In other words, volunteering could be exploitative in nature.

Just because community-based organizations are implicated in immigrants' labor market positioning and in the perpetuation of existing social and economic hierarchies in Canada, it does not mean that they have not played a critical role in immigrant services. Historically some of these organizations have been advocates for immigrants (e.g., Amin, 1987). Recent studies have also pointed out that immigrant services and service organizations may constitute spaces of critical change. For instance, Gibb, Hamdon, and Jamal (2008), using the postcolonial lens of liminality, argued that immigrant services organizations may afford a space through which immigrant women negotiate identities, create new knowledge, and forge new conceptions of communities. The women-led organizations they focused on, for instance, were able to interrupt the instrumentalism of immigrant services programs by offering some unstructured spaces of learning and connecting. The service workers they interviewed also demonstrated critical consciousness of the deficit and remedial discourse that is dominant in the services sector. In another study, Guo and Guo (2009), through four case studies, argued that immigrant services organizations, specifically, the Chinese ethnic organizations they studied, have provided accessible community-based adult education and prepared immigrants to be independent and productive citizens. Their arguments were made from the perspective of adult education for social action and inclusive citizenship. Their case studies demonstrated that ethnic communities, rather than being hindrance to immigrants' integration process (cf. Fitzpatrick, 1919), could be turned into important sites to foster emancipatory social action.

Conclusion

To end this paper, I turn to the work of Maitra and Maitra (2013). Using the lens of *standing-reserve* conceptualized by Heidegger, they suggested that in the context of modern governmentality, employment training programs often serve as "circulating mediums of subject formation demanded by the imperatives and contingent conditions of capitalist development across the globe" (p. 249). In other words, while producing particular kinds of labor, training and employment programs also necessarily produce subjects, be they citizen subjects or consumerist subjects. In view of this insight, this chapter has significant implications for adult educators involved in immigrant services. In particular, this chapter laid bare the diverse and sometimes contradictory roles that immigrant training services may play in inducting immigrants to the host labor market. It also shows that, although implicated in the production of segmented labor market, immigrant services may nonetheless play a critical role in the empowerment of immigrants and immigrant communities. In this regard, I wish to suggest that a participatory mode of governance could be a means of turning immigrant services into a radical space of change and learning for immigrants.

New Directions for Adult and Continuing Education • DOI: 10.1002/ace

Although promoting the participatory mode of governance, by no means does the chapter downplay the institutional constraints that trainers and educators need to navigate, perhaps as much as immigrants do. Nor should the chapter leave a rosy picture that participation of immigrants in the design and delivery of services is the panacea to all ills. As Lee (1993) warned many years ago, organizing with immigrant women (and by extension, all immigrants) is a mission fused with politics and power struggles. There is a continued need for adult educators and researchers to engage in critical analysis of institutional practices. Meanwhile, it is also imperative for us to note, celebrate, and learn from instances where individual empowerment and social change take place. Further, to move beyond instrumentalism policymakers and practitioners in immigrant services may start experimenting with the participatory mode of governance. By involving immigrants in the management and delivery of programs, the immigrant service sector could contribute to immigrant empowerment and citizenship building as well as social change at large.

References

Amin, N. (1987). *A preliminary history of settlement work in Ontario: 1900–present*. Ottawa, ON: Ministry of Citizenship, Citizen Development Branch. Retrieved from http://ceris .metropolis.net/Virtual%20Library/other/amim1.html

Andrew, C., & Hima, R. A. (2011). Federal immigration policy. In E. Tolley & R. Young (Eds.), *Immigrant settlement policy in Canadian Municipalities* (pp. 49–72). Montreal, PQ: McGill-Queen's University Press.

Canadian Council for Refugees. (1998). *Best settlement practices: Settlement services for refugees and immigrants in Canada*. Quebec, PQ: Canadian Council for Refugees.

Canadian Council for Refugees. (2000). *Canadian national settlement services standards framework*. Quebec, PQ: Canadian Council for Refugees. Retrieved from http://ccrweb.ca /sites/ccrweb.ca/files/static-files/standards.htm

Cervatiuc, A., & Ricento, T. (2012). Curriculum meta-orientations in the language instruction for newcomers to Canada program. *The Canadian Journal for the Study of Adult Education, 24*(2), 17–31.

Citizenship and Immigration Canada (CIC). (2001). *Immigration and refugee protection act*. Ottawa, ON: Government of Canada. Retrieved from http://laws-lois.justice.gc.ca /eng/acts/I-2.5/page-1.html

Citizenship and Immigration Canada (CIC). (2011). *Evaluation of the immigrant settlement and adaption program (ISAP)*. Ottawa, ON: Government of Canada. Retrieved from http://www.cic.gc.ca/english/resources/evaluation/isap/2011/appendixC.asp

Esses, V. M., & Gardner, R. C. (1996). Multiculturalism in Canada: Context and current status. *Canadian Journal of Behavioral Science, 28*(3), 145–152.

Fitzpatrick, A. (1919). *Handbook for new Canadians*. Toronto, ON: Ryerson Press.

Friesen, M. R. (2011). Immigrants' integration and career development in the professional engineering workplace in the context of social and cultural capital. *Engineering Studies, 3*(2), 79–100.

Gibb, T., Hamdon, E., & Jamal, Z. (2008). Re/claiming agency: Learning, liminality and immigrant service organizations. *Journal of Contemporary Issues in Education, 3*(1), 4–16.

Guo, S., & Guo, Y. (2009). Spaces/places: Exploring the possibilities and boundaries of community-based adult education for recent immigrants to Canada. In S. Carpenter, M. Laiken, & S. Mojab (Eds.), *Proceedings of the 28th National Conference of the Canadian*

Association for the Study of Adult Education (CASAE) (pp. 108–114). Ottawa, ON: Carleton University.

Integration Branch. (2001). *Immigrant integration in Canada: Policy objectives, program delivery and challenges*. Retrieved from http://atwork.settlement.org/downloads/atwork/Immigrant_Integration_in_Canada_discussion_paper_Hauck_May01.pdf

Lee, J. (1993). Organizing with immigrant women: A critique of community development in adult education. *Canadian Journal for in the Study of Adult Education, 7*(2), 19–42.

Maitra, S., & Maitra, S. (2013). The production of neoliberal subjects through employment training programs: A comparative analysis of workers' training programs in Kolkata and Toronto. In S. Brigham (Ed.), *Proceedings of the 31st National Conference of the Canadian Association for the Study of Adult Education (CASAE)* (pp. 241–247). Waterloo, ON: Wilfrid Laurier University and the University of Waterloo.

Mojab, S. (1999). De-skilling immigrant women. *Canadian Women Studies, 19*(3), 123–128.

Ng, R. (1988). *The documentary construction of "immigrant women" in Canada*. East Lansing, MI: Office of Women in International Development, Michigan State University.

Omidvar, R. (2001, June). *Social inclusion: A new vision of immigrant settlement in Canada*. Speech presented at the National Settlement Conference, Kingston, ON.

Omidvar, R., & Richmond, T. (2003). *Immigrant settlement and social inclusion in Canada*. Toronto, ON: Laidlaw Foundation. Retrieved from http://maytree.com/PDF_Files/SummaryImmigrantSettlementAndSocialInclusion2003.pdf

Richmond, T., & Shields, J. (2005). NGO-government relations and immigration services: Contradictions and challenges. *Journal of International Migration and Integration, 6*(3/4), 513–526.

Schugurensky, D., Slade, B., & Luo, Y. (2005). *Seeking "Canadian experience": The informal learning of new immigrants as volunteer workers*. Paper presented at the 24th Annual Conference of CASAE (Canadian Association for the Study of Adult Education), London, Ontario.

Scott, K., Selbee, K., & Reed, P. (2001). *Making connections: Social and civic engagement among Canadian immigrants*. Canadian Council on Social Development. Retrieved from http://volunteer.ca/content/making-connections-social-and-civic-engagement-among-canadian-immigrants

Sedef, A. (1999). Neo-liberalism, state restructuring and immigration: Changes in Canadian policies in the 1990s. *Journal of Canadian Studies, 34*(2), 31–56.

Slade, B. (2012). "From high skill to high school": Illustrating the process of deskilling immigrants through reader's theatre and institutional ethnography. *Qualitative Inquiry, 18*(5), 401–413.

Stasiulis, D., Hughes, C., & Amery, Z. (2011). From government to multilevel governance of immigrant settlement in Ontario's city-regions. In E. Tolley & R. Young (Eds.), *Immigrant settlement policy in Canadian municipalities* (pp. 73–147). Montreal, PQ: McGill-Queen's University Press.

Tastsoglou, E., & Preston, V. (2005). Gender, immigration and labour market integration: Where we are and what we still need to know. *Atlantis, 30*(1), 46–59.

Tolley, E., & Young, R. (Eds.). (2011). *Immigrant settlement policy in Canadian municipalities*. Montreal, PQ: McGill-Queen's University Press.

Van Kleef, J., & Werqin, P. (2013). PLAR in nursing: Implications of situated learning, communities of practice and consequential transition theories for recognition. *Journal of International Migration and Integration, 14*(4), 651–669.

HONGXIA SHAN *is an assistant professor in the Department of Educational Studies at the University of British Columbia, Canada.*

New Directions for Adult and Continuing Education • DOI: 10.1002/ace

Like the immigrant clients they serve, service providers have been over-looked in adult education literature, yet their roles are crucial for addressing the serious concerns of refugees and refugee claimants who flee their home countries hoping to find safe refuge in another country.

Informal Adult Learning and Emotion Work of Service Providers for Refugee Claimants

Susan M. Brigham, Catherine Baillie Abidi, Evangelia Tastsoglou, Elizabeth Lange

Significant environmental, political, economic, and social changes are occurring globally with increased intensity. Transnational migration is one phenomenon that is not only a response to global changes but itself generates global change. Migration is rarely an easy or simple process, but forced migration is fraught with risks, stress, unique vulnerabilities, and enduring precariousness. Persecution is a lived reality within the context of forced migration, resulting in people fleeing their home countries hoping to find safe refuge in another. People seeking asylum have heightened vulnerabilities due to their lack of refugee status and are often the least served groups of migrants. Given their often traumatic circumstances, refugee claimants (also known as asylum seekers) are in need of a range of settlement services, not the least of which include specialized services, such as legal aid, counseling, and mental health care (Yu, Ouellet, & Warmington, 2007). Service providers play a critical role in the lives of refugee claimants.

Like the immigrant clients they serve, service providers have been overlooked in adult education literature, yet their roles, concerns, and educational and training needs are crucial for addressing the serious issues of refugee claimants. Given the deficient literature on refugees and immigrant service providers in the adult education field, we provide a brief description of the context of refugee claimants, mainly in Canada and the United States. We then explore the role of adult education in the working lives of a group of service providers. As there is so little written on service providers who serve refugee claimants, we draw on a qualitative study that analyzed immigrant service providers' learning experiences as they go about their work of supporting refugee claimants in the Atlantic Canada region. We focus on the emotion work and the informal adult learning processes involved in negotiating shifting

New Directions for Adult and Continuing Education, no. 146, Summer 2015 © 2015 Wiley Periodicals, Inc.
Published online in Wiley Online Library (wileyonlinelibrary.com) • DOI: 10.1002/ace.20129

systems and services with refugee claimants. We conclude with recommendations for theory, research, policy, and practice in the field of adult education toward the goal of improving the experiences of refugee claimants and the capacities of service providers.

Context

A refugee is someone who, because of a "well-founded fear of being persecuted" due to his/her race, religion, or national origin, membership of a particular social group or political opinion, is unable or unwilling because of such fear, to return to his/her home country (United Nations [UN] General Assembly, 1951, p. 14). A refugee claimant is someone who is seeking international protection but his/her claim has not yet been determined. The protection of refugees was enshrined in the Geneva Convention of 1951 in response to the large number of European refugees following World War II. It was designed as a tool to protect the human rights of refugees through fundamental principles such as nondiscrimination and nonpenalization and it is meant to ensure shared global responsibility in caring for internationally displaced populations (Hathaway, 2005). The convention details the rights and responsibilities of states who are signatories to the convention, including refraining from punishing refugees for illegal entry (Article 31; UN General Assembly, 1951).

Globally, refugee claimants face a decreasing humanitarian response and a more highly securitized political climate, despite rising numbers since 2002 (United Nations High Commission for Refugees [UNHCR], 2013b). Since the Cold War ended, and particularly after 9/11, refugee movements have increasingly been portrayed as a threat to security (Rottman, Fariss, & Poe, 2009). This perception has led to what is referred to as a securitization of migration, as nation–states, concerned with protecting "the welfare systems of mass society" against the "the spontaneous circulation of non-insured global surplus life" (Duffield, 2007, p. 191), tighten control of their borders. Economic pressures and the rise of neoliberal economic policy internationally have also contributed to significant shifts in refugee policy, including increased deterrence through detention and new visa regimes, reduced acceptance rates as well as reduced provisions for basic needs (Gibney, 2004). "The restrictive treatment of asylum-seekers and illegal immigrants has also been more or less legitimized by widespread perceptions that the majority of claims are not genuine or that asylum-seekers are abusing asylum and welfare systems" (Boswell, 2011, p. 65).

Countries in the global South host four fifths of all refugees (UNHCR, 2012), in the movement that is known as South–South migration. In 2012, over 893,000 people applied for asylum around the world. In 2013, the United States received a record number of refugee claims when 88,400 people sought protection; up by 25% from the previous year (UNHCR, 2013a). Similarly, in Europe and Australia, refugee claims increased by 32% and 54% respectively from 2012 to 2013 (UNHCR, 2013a). However, in contrast, the number of new asylum applications in Canada was down by 50% in 2013 from the previous year (UNHCR, 2013a).

The acceptance of refugees in Canada has slid from 23.2% of annual immigrants in 1986 when it won the UN Nansen Medal for its humanitarian response to refugees, down to 9.1% in 2012 (Citizenship and Immigration Canada [CIC], 2012). Furthermore, refugee claimants in Canada have been significantly affected by the stark policy shifts over the past few years, from penalties for "illegal entry" (Kissoon, 2010) to an erosion of access to funded services due to a "lack of status" (Dyck & Dossa, 2007). Similarly, although the United States was the second largest recipient country of asylum claims among 44 industrial nations monitored by UNHCR (2014), Rottman, Fariss, and Poe (2009) argue that "immigrants deserving of asylum in the US have faced unnecessary and in some cases inhumane hardship" following the events of 9/11 (p. 4). Furthermore, Rosenblum and Salehyan (2004) claim that although U.S. asylum practices are embedded with normative, human rights protections, "norms often fail to constrain policy makers" who develop asylum policies that highly correlate with national trade and security interests (p. 685). In sum, "if the provision of protection for refugees is its central goal, then the system of asylum offered by Western states is currently in deep crisis" (Gibney, 2004, p. 229).

Gaps in the Literature

Although there is increasing interest among adult educators in North America for exploring migration issues, most studies have tended to focus on language learning and credential recognition for workplace integration (see, for example, Adamuti-Trache & Sweet, 2010; Guo, 2009; Ullman, 2010; Walsh, Brigham, & Wang, 2011; Wrigley, Chen, White, & Soroui, 2009). There is limited adult education literature focusing on the experiences of refugees (see Magro & Ghorayshi, 2011; Yu et al., 2007), particularly refugee claimants as a specific yet diverse population (Cohen, 2008). When refugees are mentioned, the lack of consideration for the heterogeneity of refugees is another glaring omission. Additionally, because immigrant service providers play a vital role in assisting newcomers in their host countries (Burstein & Esses, 2012; Gibb & Hamdon, 2010), our study of how they learn to navigate shifting policies and systems, and the emotion work involved while supporting refugee claimants, makes an important contribution. Our study is based on interviews and focus groups with 14 research participants who work for immigrant service organizations in Atlantic Canada.

Our chapter is then informed by an empirical study that broadly focused on policies and practices related to refugee claimants in Canada, with a particular focus on Atlantic Canada. This region is predominantly rural, which makes this research context unique. It consists of four provinces: Prince Edward Island, New Brunswick, Nova Scotia, and Newfoundland and Labrador, all of which suffer from high unemployment, decreasing population

New Directions for Adult and Continuing Education • DOI: 10.1002/ace

due to outmigration, an aging population, and low birth rates. As a way of increasing population and stimulating economic growth, all four provincial governments are looking to immigration as a solution. Yet, whereas 20.6% of all Canadians were immigrants in 2011, the highest proportion among the G8 countries (Statistics Canada, 2011), only 3.5% of Atlantic Canadians are immigrants (Akbari, Lynch, McDonald, & Rankaduwa, 2007). Out of the immigrants in 2012, there were only 134 refugee claimants in Atlantic Canada (CIC, 2012). Such small numbers of refugee claimants inevitably affect the infrastructure, practices, and perceptions of policy by service providers.

Refugee Claimant Service Providers and Adult Learning

Here we focus on two themes from the findings: the informal adult learning of service providers and the role of emotions in their work.

Informal Adult Learning. Providing service to refugee claimants in Canada requires a diversity of skills, abilities, and sustained tenacity. Although refugee claimants share a common experience of trauma and forced migration, the needs of each person vary based on multiple factors including gender, race, education, and the duration in which the forced migration(s) occurred (slow onset or fast forced migration). Combining the diversity of needs, vulnerabilities, abilities, and resources of refugee claimants with the increasingly restrictive federal refugee policies results in the need for continuous learning and navigation of systems and services. One participant describes this process as having "no formula or set way of servicing every client. Every person is different regarding the needs they have, so really at first it's kind of assessing what the person needs and we go from there." Embedded within this community-based frontline work are opportunities for learning that contribute to the everyday practice of service providers.

Polanyi (1966, cited in McGivney, 2006) suggests that "while learning is an important dimension of the activities of many voluntary and community organizations, it is often tacit and a by-product of other objectives" (p. 13). Jeffs and Smith (2005) build on this notion and describe learning as going beyond "a memory that we label as knowledge; it is also the way we search for understanding. It is something that we do" (p. 17). This is particularly evident in workplace learning where the learning taking place is often concealed in the workplace activities (McGivney, 2006). Our findings show that informal learning within the workplace significantly contributes to immigrant service providers' understandings of the vulnerabilities and settlement needs of refugee claimants and that these learning and teaching opportunities are taking place in the everyday activities of their working lives. For example, one participant states:

> Sometimes . . . I get a call from the hospital regarding a client, and then I end up talking with the nurse or the social worker for an hour about refugee claimants, or the difference between a claimant and a sponsored refugee.

New Directions for Adult and Continuing Education • DOI: 10.1002/ace

Another participant explains:

> a lot of settlement work is housing-related. You spend an inordinate amount of
> time trying to, not just secure housing, but also communicate with landlords,
> and try to mediate difficulties that come up.

The rapidly changing policies and legal frameworks guiding work in refugee settlement result in the need for service providers to constantly engage in learning and teaching in order to provide support to refugee claimants. The participants discuss how the onus is placed on service providers to maintain familiarity with constantly shifting policies that lack clarity. Furthermore, the participants express their frustration with the lack of communication and collaboration with and among government personnel in the development and implementation of refugee policy. The service providers' direct knowledge of settlement experiences of refugee claimants is not valued or taken up in relation to current refugee policymaking and execution. As McGivney (2006) suggests, an "overriding priority given to formal learning in policy and the stress on qualifications as a proxy for skills, lead to a significant undervaluing of the skills and knowledge people derive from other means" (p. 18).

Our findings also indicate that service providers' awareness and understanding of emerging migration policies largely correlate with their experiences working directly with refugee claimants. However, many Atlantic region participants work with a small number of claimants which means they often have fewer opportunities to become familiar with the specific workings and impacts of federal policies, unlike service providers working in locations with larger populations of refugee claimants. Six of the 14 participants suggest that they have limited understanding of the newest legislation. One participant states: "We're not up to speed on . . . I have, seen little bits and pieces of the legislation. But to be honest with you, I have not looked at it in detail. We're too damn busy delivering services every day."

Navigating changing federal and provincial policies and service provisions for refugee claimants is described by all participants as an exhausting experience. The participants discuss their frustrations and concerns about inefficiencies, the lack of intergovernmental communication and collaboration, and the lack of clarity in the policies. For example, one participant explains:

> I think it's more about who does what, and the lack of understanding that exists about whose responsibility it is. You know, we're trying to get some kind of support and we've got both levels of government not knowing what their responsibilities are, and saying, Well we don't do that. When in fact they do, and they just don't know. So it's about knowledge and understanding, and respecting existing policies and protocols.

Based on a study exploring the practices of the Canadian immigrant settlement sector, Burstein and Esses (2012) argue that "individual ministries know a great deal about their own programs, but less about those offered by other ministries, and far less about those offered by other jurisdictions. As a result, the ability to combine programs . . . constitutes a strategic advantage of the settlement sector" (p. 21). Participants from all four provinces find that they are regularly teaching provincial and federal personnel on policy-related issues, policies that they have had to navigate themselves with their colleagues and with their clients. The participants describe their educator role with and between federal and provincial personnel as frustrating and repetitive, a "bureaucratic nightmare." They further state: "It's just one of those things that seems quite simple, but doesn't seem to happen . . . there doesn't seem to be institutional knowledge."

> Not having to tell other departments how to do their job, not having to explain what a refugee claimant is, again and again. That's probably the hardest thing for me. I mean, I still, I'll do it and I'll keep calling and will advocate for the client a hundred percent, but it's just kind of one of those things where you go, wow, this could be so simple, yet they make it so complicated.

Burstein and Esses (2012) conclude that

> service provider organizations acquire their integrative skills on-the-job, by virtue of attempting to solve problems encountered by newcomers and their families. This ability to combine and coordinate different programs is not something that government ministries do well. (p. 21)

The participants contrast their own learning experiences and the construction of knowledge through their service work with the lack of engagement of government personnel. The participants see this teaching role as vital to their ability to support refugee claimant clients but it is also a challenge that "slows down the process of getting the aid that [claimants] need."

Emotion Work. "The experience of work is saturated with feeling" (Ashforth & Humphrey, 1993, p. 98). This is particularly true for work that involves providing care and service to others. Our participants consistently indicate there is an intensity of emotions involved in providing service for persons who are fleeing persecution and whose access to protection is determined by a lone Immigration and Refugee Board (IRB) member.

Hochschild (1979) first introduced the notion of *emotion work*, which is "the act of *trying* to change in degree or quality an emotion or feeling" (p. 561). This work involves evoking and/or suppressing feelings in oneself, using cognitive, bodily, or expressive techniques. At times this requires that we engage in deep acting to convince ourselves that we feel a certain way, because we believe we should, given the circumstances, even when we don't feel that way. Our research participants shared examples of deep acting when referring to a notion of professionalism that involves a complex negotiation of emotions. For example, a participant notes: "I try not to cry because you know, you're at the IRB, you want to be tough and stuff like that." In another example, during a conversation between two participants, they allude to a notion of professionalism that involves a deliberate detachment from emotions:

A: But it's obviously such an emotional procedure and everything around the refugee claim is so traumatic sometimes and raw, that you know you can't be too detached . . . .

B: Be professional, yet compassionate . . .

A: And then for us as well, knowing that sometimes we're going to have to say good-bye to someone, and there's nothing more that we can do.

B: [You have] to try to detach yourself sometimes from all of the emotions, and every day has so many ups and downs, and it's really difficult . . .

A: It's important . . . for the job, to be able to have that detachment because when you don't have it, then you can't make . . . informed decisions, informed and detached, professional decisions.

The informal learning referred to previously involves attention to the social rules found in every workplace, including organizations offering services to refugee claimants. These involve feeling rules, emotion management, and emotive experience (Hochschild, 1979). These learned and often unspoken rules dictate how we should try to feel or not feel and how we should display or control our emotions as deemed appropriate in any given situation (Hochschild, 1979). Adhering to workplace feeling rules involves obeisance to guidelines that are usually not of our own making (not personally or individually) and they may not be in our own best interest. But we are often compelled to follow such rules in the interest of upholding the ideal of professionalism in a workplace. In the previous example, detachment is seen to be the best way to be professional; however, deep acting and obeying feeling rules that may not be in our own best interest can lead to a sense of alienation, of not being true to oneself and one's ethics, leaving one doubtful of one's own ability to authentically feel what is appropriate at the right time, the right place, and with certain people.

As service providers, our research participants are the mediators between the claimant and the bureaucratic state. In these roles they are engaged in emotion work, whereas the state, policy makers, and bureaucrats can in effect be disengaged from the emotive experiences and face-to-face encounters of service providers working directly with refugee claimants. Service providers play the role of the understanding, patient supporter who faces the varied emotions of their clients as this example demonstrates:

D: Yeah, the majority of these people who arrive in container ships, when they get out of detention they're very frustrated . . . They're upset, they kind of want to take it out, they need to release the tension and the stress, and everything that's happened. And you know, we often are the recipients of that frustration, and it's difficult because then it's hard to form a respectful relationship. And they become even more vulnerable.

E: Sometimes they just burn their bridges, and we have to close files because of inappropriateness or violent behavior, things like that.

D: So that perpetuates their vulnerability. Increases it ... It's so challenging for us the service providers, but for them as well ... You need to understand that we're your advocates to get you through the system, and it's the system that's long. We're on your side. But it's also people who come from countries and backgrounds where there's a lot of distrust as well, so that's a normal reaction.

This self-defeating action makes emotion work even more complicated.

For our research participants, their work frequently involves disheartenment and frustration usually as a result of not being able to fully assist their clients. For example, one participant states, "our hearts break when we talk to somebody and we have to kind of ask them to go away because there is nothing to help them here." Examples of the emotional toll of this work were illustrated as feelings of empathy and heartache for refugees who are experiencing "desperation," "separation of families," "instability," and for "women who fled without their children." Others express frustrations over the lack of options they have to support refugee claimants in their communities and the challenges of witnessing the aftermath of a negative refugee board decision. "Not being able to help" was the strongest source of the emotional burden of the service providers' work.

The research participants also note the impact of such work on their personal lives. For example:

I'd like to be an idealist, but ... when it comes down to it, am I going to stay here until nine o'clock at night and maybe make a difference on the file of this person, who may or may not be deported, or am I going to go to supper with my parents? Like when it's that decision, it's so hard to make. But then, it is a cumulative effect of craziness.

They referred to the benefits of sharing their experiences and emotional reactions with other service providers. In one city a small group organizes regular meetings in which they discuss their work and provide support to each other. Still others referred to wine as a means of helping them cope or as a strategy for continuing in this work. Although the comments about wine were often said with a laugh, they indicate that drinking wine was an opportunity to unwind at the end of the day. Other strategies include working more intensely and trying to stay emotionally detached.

Although we recognize the limitations of Hochschild's seminal work, including not sufficiently distinguishing between the private self and the public self (Bolton, 2005, cited in Shan, 2012), clarifying the degree of managerial control over the emotions of workers (Bolton & Boyd, 2003, cited in Shan, 2012), or explaining workers' agency and resistance (Brook, 2009, cited in Shan, 2012), we value the attention brought to the relational power dynamics of emotion that is rooted in work and daily negotiation processes. For our participants, emotion work is a critical part of their daily informal learning and their work with refugee claimants. It also shows how our participants' emotion work affects their personal lives, particularly their own emotional health and social well-being.

Conclusion

Despite rising global numbers, refugee claimants are faced with an increased deterrence and securitized environment that are threatening the existing system of asylum provided by Western countries. Refugee claimants are generally the least served and most socially excluded group of immigrants in a host country. Yet in the adult education literature, refugees and most especially refugee claimants receive little attention.

Our study demonstrates that this crisis in the system of asylum is evident in the perspective of service providers, who are the advocates for refugee claimants and mediators between claimants and the bureaucratic state. Service providers are engaged in informal on-the-job learning, acquired through their advocacy work and through the challenge of navigating complex systems and services. Our research participants also highlight the intensity of emotions involved in providing service for persons who are fleeing persecution and how emotion work affects their public and private lives. Our examination of the relational power dynamics of emotional labor uncovers the ways in which our research participants negotiate and balance emotions for the benefit of their clients, their own sense of professionalism, and in turn the state.

Service providers point to the need for changes in their work environments, including greater financial, ideological, and educational support from the state. The organizations for which service providers work are generally understaffed, resulting in insufficient time and energy to support the needs of refugee claimants. Participants expressed the wish for a changed prorefugee political climate that would facilitate their work and would be more in agreement with Canada's officially humanitarian ideological discourse.

We assert that adult educators need to be attentive to the plight of refugee claimants, as their basic living circumstances and learning needs are unique. Other changes highlighted by service providers are increased educational opportunities to keep abreast of new knowledge, for example, of legislation and policy changes, which should be provided at regular intervals by federal and provincial immigration officials. Additionally, improved access to information and greater communication between service workers and immigration officers at all levels of government are felt to be needed, with a clear delineation of jurisdiction for various levels of government in relation to specific services and protection of refugee claimants.

New Directions for Adult and Continuing Education • DOI: 10.1002/ace

With a dearth of research in this area, we recommend that further research be conducted with service providers, refugee claimants, and policy makers to understand how policies that govern refugee claimant issues are taken up in various contexts and how they affect the quality of life for refugee claimants as well as those who provide services to them. At the same time the focus on emotion work through an organizational lens, connecting emotions to specific kinds of labor as well as to organizational values such as power and social justice, would be a valuable contribution to the adult education literature.

The findings of our study point to several implications for practitioners. Recognizing the emotional labor involved in working as service providers and the impact it has on their lives, practitioners must work to create spaces and opportunities to attend to their emotional, mental, and spiritual needs individually and collectively. This might entail regularly reaching out to other service providers in the region or beyond in face-to-face or distance formats to engage in dialogue, reflect on their practice, support one another, find ways to advocate not only for their clients but for themselves, and work to institute appropriate changes. A professional association for service providers who work with refugees and refugee claimants may be a way to further their interests and those of the public and contribute to the ongoing professional development of service providers as well as the continuing education of this group of workers. Such an association could also direct research agendas and offer research opportunities to community-based and academic partners.

References

Adamuti-Trache, M., & Sweet, R. (2010). Adult immigrants' participation in Canadian education and training. *Canadian Journal for the Study of Adult Education, 22*(2), 1–26.

Akbari, A., Lynch, S., McDonald, J. T., & Rankaduwa, W. (2007). *Socioeconomic & demographic profiles of immigrants in Atlantic Canada*. Halifax, NS: Atlantic Metropolis Centre.

Ashforth, B. E., & Humphrey, R. H. (1993). Emotional labor in service roles—the influence of identity. *Academy of Management Review, 18*, 88–115.

Boswell, C. (2011). *European migration policies in flux: Changing patterns of inclusion and exclusion*. Oxford, UK: Blackwell Publishing.

Burstein, M., & Esses, V. (2012). *Study of innovative and promising practices within the immigrant settlement sector*. Ottawa, ON: Canadian Immigrant Settlement Sector Alliance.

Citizenship and Immigration Canada (CIC). (2012). *Facts and figures 2011: Immigration overview*. Ottawa, ON: Citizenship and Immigration Canada.

Cohen, J. (2008). Safe in our hands? A study of suicide and self-harm in asylum seekers. *Journal of Forensic and Legal Medicine, 15*(4), 235–244.

Duffield, M. (2007). *Development security and unending war: Governing the world of peoples*. Cambridge, UK: Polity Press.

Dyck, I., & Dossa, P. (2007). Place, health and home: Gender and migration in the construction of healthy space. *Health and Place, 13*(3), 691–701.

Gibb, T., & Hamdon, E. (2010). Moving across borders: Immigrant women's encounters with globalization, the knowledge economy and lifelong learning. *International Journal of Lifelong Education, 29*(2), 185–200.

Gibney, M. (2004). *The ethics and politics of asylum: Liberal democracy and the response to refugees.* Cambridge, UK: Cambridge University Press.

Guo, S. (2009). Difference, deficiency, and devaluation: Tracing the roots of non/recognition of foreign credentials for immigrant professionals in Canada. *Canadian Journal for the Study of Adult Education, 22*(1), 37–52.

Hathaway, J. (2005). *The rights of refugees under international law.* Cambridge, UK: Cambridge University Press.

Hochschild, A. R. (1979). Emotion work, feeling rules, and social structure. *The American Journal of Sociology, 85*(3), 551–575.

Jeffs, T., & Smith, M. (2005). *Informal education: Conversation, democracy, and learning.* Nottingham, UK: Educational Heretics Press.

Kissoon, P. (2010). *(Dis)advantages of illegality* (MBC Working Paper, 10–11). Vancouver, BC: Metropolis British Columbia.

Magro, K., & Ghorayshi, P. (2011). *Adult refugees and newcomers in the inner city of Winnipeg: Promising pathways for transformative learning.* Winnipeg, MB: Canadian Centre for Policy Alternatives. Retrieved from https://www.policyalternatives.ca/publications/reports/adult-refugees-and-newcomers-inner-city-winnipeg#sthash.rAa5EdUj.dpuf

McGivney, V. (2006). Informal learning: The challenge for research. In R. Edwards, J. Gallacher, & S. Whittaker (Eds.), *Learning outside the academy: International research perspectives on lifelong learning* (pp. 11–23). London, UK: Routledge.

Rosenblum, M., & Salehyan, I. (2004). Norms and interests in US asylum enforcement. *Journal of Peace Research, 41*(6), 677–699.

Rottman, A., Fariss, C., & Poe, S. (2009). The path to asylum in the US and the determinants for who gets in and why. *International Migration Review, 43*(1), 3–34.

Shan, H. (2012). Learning to "fit in": The emotional work of Chinese immigrant engineers in Canada. *Journal of Workplace Learning, 24*(5), 351–364.

Statistics Canada. (2011). *Immigration and ethno-cultural diversity in Canada.* Retrieved from https://www12.statcan.gc.ca/nhs-enm/2011/as-sa/99-010-x/99-010-x2011001-eng.cfm

Ullman, C. (2010). The connections among immigration, nation building, and adult education English as a second language instruction in the United States. *Adult Learning, 21*(1–2), 4–8.

United Nations (UN) General Assembly. (1951). *Convention relating to the status of refugees* (UN, Treaty Series, 189). Retrieved from http://www.unhcr.org/refworld/docid/3be01b964.html

United Nations High Commission of Refugees (UNHCR). (2012). *UNCHR global trends 2011.* Geneva, Switzerland: Author.

United Nations High Commission of Refugees (UNHCR). (2013a). *UNHCR asylum trends 2013: Levels and trends in industrialized countries.* Geneva, Switzerland: Author.

United Nations High Commission of Refugees (UNHCR). (2013b). *Displacement: The new 21st century challenge.* Geneva, Switzerland: Author.

United Nations High Commission of Refugees (UNHCR). (2014). *UNHCR asylum trends first half of 2014: Levels and trends in industrial countries.* Geneva, Switzerland: Author.

Walsh, S., Brigham, S., & Wang, Y. (2011). Internationally educated female teachers in the neoliberal context: Their labour market and teacher certification experiences in Canada. *Teaching and Teacher Education, 27*, 657–665.

Wrigley, H. S., Chen, J., White, S., & Soroui, J. (2009). Assessing the literacy skills of adult immigrants and adult English language learners. In C. Larrotta & A. K. Brooks (Eds.), *New Directions for Adult and Continuing Education: No. 121. Bringing community to the adult ESL classroom* (pp. 5–24). San Francisco, CA: Jossey-Bass.

Yu, S., Ouellet, E., & Warmington, A. (2007). Refugee integration in Canada: A survey of empirical evidence and existing services. *Refuge, 24*(2), 17–34.

SUSAN M. BRIGHAM is an associate professor in the Faculty of Education in the Graduate Studies of Lifelong Learning program at Mount Saint Vincent University, Canada. She is also an associate editor of the Canadian Journal for the Study of Adult Education.

CATHERINE BAILLIE ABIDI is a PhD candidate in the Faculty of Education at St. Francis Xavier University, Canada.

EVANGELIA TASTSOGLOU is a professor in the Department of Sociology and Criminology at Saint Mary's University, Canada.

ELIZABETH LANGE is an associate professor in the Department of Adult Education at St. Francis Xavier University, Canada, and is also an associate editor for the Canadian Journal for the Study of Adult Education.

New Directions for Adult and Continuing Education • DOI: 10.1002/ace

4

This chapter examines current issues in English as Second Language (ESL) policies and programs for adult immigrants in Canada from a critical multiculturalism perspective.

Language Policies and Programs for Adult Immigrants in Canada: Deconstructing Discourses of Integration

Yan Guo

Research shows that language is one of the most outstanding challenges facing adult immigrants in transitioning to a new society (Guo, 2013). Adult education is often charged with the responsibility of providing English as a Second Language (ESL) programs to help newcomers upgrade their language and skills. In Canada, policies on immigration, bilingualism, and multiculturalism have all interacted with larger global trends to produce the current state of ESL programs for adult immigrants. Accordingly, these three policy areas are central to any discussion of language programs for adult immigrants. This chapter begins with a discussion of these three policy areas, followed by a historical overview of language education in Canada and within the current policy context. The last part discusses implications for language education for adult immigrants.

Immigration Context

Immigration to Canada since the late 19th century was governed by a state policy that defined and welcomed a particular class of desirable immigrants and restricted the entry of those considered undesirable (Li, 2003a). From 1867 to 1895, Canada welcomed immigration from certain people of European origin, especially from the United Kingdom and the United States. Severe restrictions were placed on immigrants from Asia. From 1896 to 1914 when immigrants from the United Kingdom and Western Europe could not meet labor demands, Canada began to allow Eastern and Southern Europe immigrants, such as Poles, Ukrainians, Hutterites, and Doukhobors to immigrate. Asians and other non-Whites were seen as those "unlikely to assimilate" (Manpower and Immigration Canada, 1974, p. 10) "because of their superficial racial and cultural differences" (Li, 2003a, p. 19). Canada used race as

New Directions for Adult and Continuing Education, no. 146, Summer 2015 © 2015 Wiley Periodicals, Inc.
Published online in Wiley Online Library (wileyonlinelibrary.com) • DOI: 10.1002/ace.20130

a basis to restrict Asians and other non-Whites. In this way, immigration has functioned as a means of cultural domination and social control. From 1915 to 1945, British and American immigrants were preferred, followed by North European and then Central Europeans (Li, 2003a). At the end of the Second World War, Canadian immigration policy continued to use ethnicity and nationality as the central criteria of immigrant selection (Li, 2003a). Between 1946 and 1955, about 87% of the immigrants came from Europe (Manpower and Immigration Canada, 1970). In the 1960s, it became clear immigrants from the traditional sources could not meet labor demands in Canada. The establishment of the point system in 1967, using prescriptive criteria based on education, occupation, language skills, and work experience, removed ethnoracial or national barriers in immigrant selection. Throughout the 1980s and 1990s governments placed greater emphasis on human capital and the economic benefits of immigration (Walsh, 2008). The point system has facilitated immigration from developing countries. By 2011, nearly 82.3% of immigrants came from Asia, Africa, the Middle East, Central and South America, and the Caribbean (Statistics Canada, 2013).

Bilingualism and Multiculturalism

The unification of Canada as a single confederation in 1867 represented a compromise between two immigrant societies—British and French—who agreed to form a polity fundamentally divided into a two-language, two-culture country (Li, 2003a). Beginning in the late 1960s, the Canadian government sought to reconstruct the character of the nation through two policy initiatives: bilingualism and multiculturalism. Bilingualism was, in part, a response to Quebec separatism (Esses & Gardner, 1996). The Official Languages Act of 1969 granted French and English equal status as official languages of Parliament and the federal government. Aboriginal languages were excluded. With the second policy, promulgated in 1971, Canada became the first country in the world to make multiculturalism an official state policy. Multiculturalism, which arose in the aftermath of the *Report of the Royal Commission on Bilingualism and Biculturalism*, was introduced as a political exercise for bolstering national unity (Fleras & Elliott, 2002). Although the French–English rift was central to the report, various minority ethnic groups, especially the Ukrainians and the Germans, argued vigorously that their language and culture were as vital to Canada's nation building as was Quebec's. The Liberal government of the day saw official multiculturalism within a bilingual framework as a compromise position that could both head off Quebec nationalism and satisfy the thirst for recognition of various ethnic groups. The commitment to multiculturalism was not only enshrined in legislation (the 1988 Canadian Multiculturalism Act), but also constitutionalized in section 27 of the *Charter of Rights and Freedoms* (1982).

Multiculturalism has a plurality of meanings. According to Kincheloe and Steinberg (1997), there are three prevailing philosophical positions that inform multicultural policies and practices: conservative, liberal, and critical.

The conservative approach presumes the superiority of Eurocentric values and beliefs, devalues immigrants' native cultures, and places uneven expectations on immigrants to conform to the norms, values, and traditions of the receiving society (Li, 2003a). The liberal position acknowledges diversity but superficially focuses on universal human race. An alternative form of liberal multiculturalism is pluralist multiculturalism, which sees differences in people and cultures. However, cultural differences are often exoticized and essentialized as ends in themselves. Multicultural discussions and practices often involve othering, listing how "they" are different from "us." Both conservative and liberal approaches to multiculturalism move attention away from systemic racism and power inequities by maintaining the superiority of a dominant group and promoting a superficial rhetoric of equality, diversity, and political correctness. By contrast, critical multiculturalism makes explicit hidden or masked structures, discourses, and relations of inequity that discriminate against one group and enhance the privileges of another. Questioning ideology is central to the critical enterprise and involves "the attempt to unearth and challenge dominant ideology and the power relations this ideology justifies" (Brookfield, 2000, p. 38).

In the past 40 years, Canada's version of multiculturalism has been praised and adopted internationally. At the same time Canada has been criticized for having "endorsed diversity in principle without actually changing in any fundamental way how power and resources [are] distributed" (Fleras & Elliott, 2002, p. 56). One of the flaws of multicultural policy lies in the separation of culture and language. Canadian bilingualism defined English and French as the official languages of Canada. This policy, by deemphasizing the languages of other cultural groups, helped to create a cultural and linguistic hierarchy in Canada. Whereas multicultural policy suggested that newcomers were free to preserve their traditional cultures, bilingualism implied the assimilation of immigrants into the cultures of the two founding races. Multiculturalism within a bilingual framework maintains White-settler hegemony while also disavowing exclusion of Aboriginal and other ethnic groups (Haque, 2012).

ESL Programs for Adult Immigrants

This section examines how the purposes of ESL programs for adult immigrants have shifted from an assimilationist stance to integration over the years from a critical multiculturalism perspective. The federal government first offered second language training for adult immigrants in 1947 (McDonald, George, Cleghorn, & Karenova, 2008). Since that time, the federal government and various ministries in each province have administered ESL programs. These programs are offered by school boards, community colleges, universities, nongovernmental organizations, and the private sector. The programs typically serve four purposes: English language training, preparation for the labor market, preparation for the citizenship test, and integration into Canadian society.

Until the early 1990s ESL programs for adult immigrants took an assimilationist approach to citizenship preparation and nation building. With the introduction of the Citizenship Act in 1947, the federal government created a series of programs, collectively known as the Citizenship Instruction and Language Textbooks, to provide ESL classes for adult immigrants (James & Burnaby, 2003). The purpose of immigrant education focused on "acquainting the immigrant into the habits, customs, and institutions of Canada" (Joshee, 1996, p. 113). The expectation was that the immigrant's language(s) and culture(s) would be replaced by English and French and the dominant Anglo-Saxon culture in Canada (Ciccarelli, 1997).

Over the years, the purpose of ESL programs for adult immigrants has shifted from an assimilationist stance to a focus on language training for employment. In 1978, the federal government, through the Canada Employment and Immigration Commission, created a national language training project as a component of the Canadian Job Strategies program. The program provided language training for adult immigrants and native Canadians who could not find employment because of their lack of proficiency in English or French. It provided a living allowance to trainees, but only heads of households, who were mostly male, were eligible. Such policy on language training was unjust in its application to immigrant women (Giles, 1988).

As a result of a court challenge sponsored by several immigrant organizations and public criticism of this discriminatory language policy, in 1986 the Canada Employment and Immigration Commission created a program called the Settlement Language Training Program (SLTP). The program provided up to 500 hours of basic language training to adults who were not destined for the labor market, primarily immigrant women (Canada Employment and Immigration Commission, 1986). The SLTP funds provided daycare and transportation to participants. Other programs, the Secretary of State Citizenship and Language Training Program and the Citizenship and Community Participation Program, prepared adult immigrants for their citizenship hearing. All of these programs were replaced by Language Instruction for Newcomers to Canada (LINC) in 1992.

LINC was the central component of the Immigration Plan for 1991–1995 that introduced the federal integration strategy (Citizenship and Immigration Canada [CIC], 2001). LINC was to support the integration of immigrants: "LINC facilitates the social, cultural and economic integration of immigrants and refugees into Canada. Included in the LINC curriculum guidelines . . . is information that helps orient newcomers to the Canadian way of life" (CIC, 2006, "Description"). This indicates a policy shift from a focus on language training for employment to a focus on language for integration. LINC introduced newcomers to "shared Canadian values, rights, and responsibilities" (Bettencourt, 2003, p. 25). The content covered in classes included Canadian laws, basic vocabulary for shopping and banking, and orientation to local services such as public transportation and housing (Bettencourt, 2003).

Immigrants and refugees in all provinces except Quebec are entitled to access to LINC programs, preferably within the first year of their arrival. Quebec established its own program for French-as-a-second-language immigrants.

New Directions for Adult and Continuing Education • DOI: 10.1002/ace

Canadian citizens are barred from LINC programs. Trainees are not usually eligible for living allowances but can apply for support for transportation and child care. They generally receive about 900 hours of instruction. LINC provides immigrants with survival language skills, a level not sufficient to access postsecondary education or meet the language demands of professional fields (Boyd & Cao, 2009).

In 2003 the federal government introduced the Enhanced Language Training (ELT) to provide a higher level of language training for the workplace. Most of the programs funded in 2003–2004 emphasized language training for specific fields (e.g., engineering, nursing) and cross-cultural communication skills, as well as the soft skills necessary for immigrants to obtain and maintain employment. In general, ELT programs are equivalent to Canadian Language Benchmark levels 7–10. These programs include classroom language instruction, unpaid work experience placement, and job search assistance. As a whole, ELT programs focus on facilitating skilled immigrants' entry into the labor market.

Emerging Trends and Issues

In the next section, current trends and issues in ESL programs for adult immigrants are explored by deconstructing discourses of integration at the level of both policy and practice, by examining problems of teaching Canadian values, and by critiquing the emphasis on employability in ESL programs.

Deconstructing Discourses of Integration. As mentioned previously, LINC was created as part of a federal integration strategy. What it is, precisely, that constitutes integration of immigrants is often taken for granted. A report of the CIC (1994), for example, explains the concept of integration as follows:

> Integration implies a political desire and commitment to encourage newcomers to adapt to Canadian society and to be received by Canadians and their institutions without requiring newcomers to abandon their cultures to conform to the values and practices of the dominant group, as long as the adherence to immigrants' cultures does not contravene Canadian laws. (p. 7)

The policy objective of integration, as stated, is a two-way process, requiring mutual adjustments by both newcomers and Canadian society. The policy stresses that integration allows newcomers to maintain their distinct cultures under multiculturalism (Li, 2003b).

In practice, however, the assessment of integration is often based on a narrow understanding and a rigid expectation of conformity of newcomers to preexisting norms and behavioral standards (Li, 2003b). Li (2003b) is skeptical about whether integration really means anything other than slow assimilation. The pattern of assimilation has been implicitly endorsed in research by measuring immigrants' "success" by how much like Canadians they can become and how quickly this can be achieved. Prior to 1960s immigrants were mainly Europeans. Since the 1970s immigrants have been mainly Asians and Africans. Changes brought to Canada in the 1980s and early 1990s challenged Canadians who have historically assumed a "White tenor" and a "Eurocentric perspective" (Mercer, 1995, pp. 171–172). Historically, immigrants "were being progressively incorporated into a collective identity and an institutional system whose symbolic character was fundamentally British, but regarded as Canadian" (Breton, 1984, p. 128). Examining policy statements, immigration debates, and academic writing, Li (2003b) argued that integration discourse endorses the assimilation of immigrants into British based Canadian norms.

Deconstructing Teaching Canadian Values. One way that the federal government's policy on integration has been implemented is through the insertion of "information on Canadian values into training programs" (Employment and Immigration Canada, 1991, p. 2). Of course what constitutes Canadian values is debatable. When LINC was first introduced, Employment and Immigration Canada contracted a company to develop a publication titled *Canada: A Source Book for Orientation, Language and Settlement Workers* (Arcturus Productions, 1991). The book defined a static version of Canadian culture based on descriptions of what Canadians do and do not do. It recommended that teachers uplift adult immigrants through the teaching of health, proper hygiene, and morals. The book was later withdrawn after it was criticized as patronizing by workers in immigrant-serving agencies (Fleming, 2003).

Despite this history, most ESL curriculum documents and teaching guidelines still tend to present Canadian culture as a national attribute consisting of sets of stable values and behavior patterns (Illieva, 2000). Sauvè (1996) argued that "we live in a society that sees itself as multicultural while continuing to be biased in favor of White, Anglo-Saxon, Christian, middle-class traditions and values" (p. 21). Similarly, Illieva (2000) illustrated how excerpts from a unit titled Department Stores in *Canadian Concepts 3*, one of the textbooks used in LINC, reflected middle-class shopping habits and values, assuming a universality of cultural experiences around shopping in Canada as well as in a student's native country.

The condescending stereotypes in the *Source Book* persist in some current ESL programs for adult immigrants. In a case study of an ESL program for adults in an immigrant-serving organization in Western Canada, Y. Guo (2009) found that immigrants felt they were expected to "think like and act like Canadians." A job-preparation workshop facilitator promoted the assimilation of immigrants to Anglo norms (Y. Guo, 2009, p. 49): "You don't think like a Chinese, an Indian or a Pakistan, or Iranian, or Iraqi, you should think like a Canadian. So you have to go out and take part in Canadian activities in Canadian life."

Immigrants are advised to "think like a Canadian." This advice assumes, first of all, that there is a shared way of thinking that can be described as "Canadian." Two implications should be noted. First, this implies that being Canadian is incompatible with an ethnic identity. Governing practices take the form of normative judgments that a particular form of conduct or behavior is essentially wrong or bad (Hunt, 1999), that is, to think like a Chinese or Iranian is to be un-Canadian. An immigrant himself, the facilitator has internalized a colonial mentality and, in turn, attempts to colonize the minds and practices of new immigrants. Such internalization supports the supremacy of White, Eurocentric norms and behaviors. Despite the official policy of multiculturalism, Canada is "dominated by the hegemonic British and the French cultural norms" (Satzewich & Liodakis, 2007, p. 123).

Deconstructing the Focus on "Employability." Another way to implement the federal government's policy on integration was to prepare immigrants for the Canadian labor market. To address the issue of the lack of Canadian experience, the ELT program made unpaid work experience part of its components. Although these programs purport to offer professional language acquisition and labor market knowledge, some service providers have attempted to mold skilled immigrants according to an ideal of the compliant worker (Soveran, 2011). Y. Guo's (2009) study of an ELT bridge-to-work program for skilled immigrants in a Western Canada city shows that the program focused on presentability and employability of immigrants for the Canadian labor market through processes such as reducing their accent, anglicizing their names, and adapting to Canadian linguistic and cultural norms.

Similarly, another study of the ELT bridge-to-work program for skilled immigrants delivered by a nonprofit immigrant-serving agency in Western Canada demonstrates that the program aimed to help immigrants understand Canadian workplace culture and fit into the workplace (Soveran, 2011). There were specific ways that the program endeavored to show the immigrants how to fit in through a cultural understanding of what it meant to be a professional in Canada. These included developing positive attitudes, self-presentation as confident, bodily comportment in conservative dress, workplace values such as the North American relationship to time, the importance of work–life balance, and building soft skills. Service providers explained that soft skills meant appropriate interpersonal relationships and communication. These included being polite and friendly, capable of teamwork, making small talks with their coworkers, and asking to join coworkers at lunch. The discourse of "fitting in" is problematic. Such discourse promotes a one-way process of integration, requiring immigrants to adapt to the Canadian workplace expectations, but there were no discussions of employment discrimination and gender inequality these immigrants faced in the Canadian labor market. In that sense, this program adopts conservative and liberal approaches to multiculturalism by endorsing conformity to the "ideal Canadian employee."

Implications for Adult Education

Current immigration and adult immigrant language policies endorse a conceptual framework of integration, but the policy in practice is assimilationist not integrationist. The ESL programs, focusing on teaching Canadian values, have failed to integrate cultural difference and diversity into language education. On the contrary, the programs have become a vehicle to assimilating immigrants into the norms of the dominant culture. The current policy directing adult immigrant English language education in Canada emphasizes human capital models, the functional goal of job preparation, and individualized skills (Gibb, 2008). ESL programs for adult immigrants have become a mechanism of neoliberal control to produce ideal workers for the Canadian labor market (Ng & Shan, 2010). Perhaps Fraser's (2009) recognitive social justice is a promising alternative to these issues.

Recognitive justice includes social goods, such as opportunity, position, and power, as well as institutional inequities (Fraser, 2009). The emphasis on equality of opportunity and participation positions integration as a non-coercive two-way process that requires mutual change by both newcomers and Canadian society. It is not just the newcomers who need to adapt to the Canadian culture. The receiving society also needs to change in order to recognize political, cultural, linguistic, and economic contributions of immigrants to Canada.

Adult educators need to adopt a critical multiculturalism approach that challenges their own deficit perspective of difference (S. Guo, 2009) and becomes cultural brokers and transformers by providing immigrants with strategies to overcome employers' racism. They can examine real issues facing immigrants, such as nonrecognition of foreign credentials, racism in hiring practices, and accent discrimination (Y. Guo, 2009; Munro, 2003). Focusing on language skills is not sufficient in the Language Instruction for Newcomers to Canada program. Rather, adult educators can help immigrants develop critical language awareness in order to contest and change practices of domination (Fairclough, 1995) and reclaim their professional knowledge.

In adult language education, the development of educational services for adult immigrants, from a recognitive justice perspective, would include immigrant knowledge and community input on the creation and implementation of appropriate programs (Fraser, 2009). One approach is to value immigrants' professional knowledge and to activate such knowledge for Canadian contexts in the Enhanced Language Training program. Immigrant professionals know the professional concepts of their fields in their native language. They may not know how to express these concepts adequately in English. Bilingual programs in both English and immigrants' native language can be offered in large metropolitan centers where many immigrants share the same native language. With the funding from the federal government, different language programs can be designed to meet different needs of the learners. Immigrant parents who want to stay at home for several years can participate in social conversation classes. Newcomers, whose goal is to find employment in the Canadian labor market, can be connected with multilingual mentors in the workplace. More senior colleagues can serve as mentors to provide on-the-job training that is similar to apprenticeship (Reitz, 2005). Mentors can share their knowledge and experience with newcomers and help them build professional and business networks. Skilled immigrants can participate in occupation-specific mentoring.

The preparation of citizenship education in ESL programs for adult immigrants, from a recognitive justice perspective, would reject the current deficit model that seeks to assimilate immigrants to the norms of the dominant culture. This perspective calls for *pluralist citizenship* that recognizes that immigrants have multiple attachments to specific languages, cultures, and values (Guo, 2010). Adult educators can incorporate immigrants' transcultural experiences into curriculum and explore the meanings of Canadian citizenship from immigrants' perspectives. It requires a transformation of policy and practice in language programs for the social inclusion of adult immigrants to take into account of plural ways of belonging, dynamic negotiations of transnational identities, and plural ways of becoming Canadians (Guo, 2010; Waterhouse, 2011).

References

Arcturus Productions. (1991). *Canada: A source book for orientation, language and settlement workers.* Ottawa, ON: Employment and Immigration Canada.

Bettencourt, E. (2003). LINC then and now: 10-year anniversary. *TESL Ontario, 29*(2), 25–28.

Boyd, M., & Cao, X. (2009). Immigrant language proficiency, earnings, and language policies. *Canadian Studies in Population, 36*(1–2), 63–86.

Breton, R. (1984). The production and allocation of symbolic resources: An analysis of the linguistic and ethnocultural fields in Canada. *Canadian Review of Sociology and Anthropology, 21*(2), 123–144.

Brookfield, S. D. (2000). The concept of critically reflective practice. In A. L. Wilson & E. R. Hayes (Eds.), *Handbook of adult and continuing education* (pp. 33–50). San Francisco, CA: Jossey-Bass.

Canada Employment and Immigration Commission. (1986). *Settlement language training program: Program description and guidelines.* Ottawa, ON: Author.

Ciccarelli, S. B. (1997). *ESL for nation-building: The origin of federally-funded ESL in Canada* (Unpublished master's thesis). University of Toronto, Toronto, Ontario, Canada.

Citizenship and Immigration Canada (CIC). (1994). *What are the key elements of a strategy for integrating newcomers into Canadian society?* The report of working group #5, 1994 Immigration Consultation. Ottawa, ON: Author.

Citizenship and Immigration Canada (CIC). (2001). *Immigrant integration in Canada: Policy objectives, program delivery and challenges.* Ottawa, ON: Author. Retrieved from http://wiki .settlementatwork.org/wiki/Immigrant_Integration_in_Canada:_Policy_Objectives,_Pro gram_Delivery_and_Challenges

Citizenship and Immigration Canada (CIC). (2006). *Major crown projects and horizontal initiatives.* Retrieved from http://www.cic.gc.ca/english/resources/publications/horizontal -2006.asp#linc

Employment and Immigration Canada. (1991). *Immigrant language training policy framework.* Ottawa, ON: Settlement Policy and Program Development.

Esses, V., & Gardner, R. C. (1996). Multiculturalism in Canada: Context and current status. *Canadian Journal of Behavioural Science, 28*(3), 145–152.

Fairclough, N. (1995). *Critical discourse analysis: The critical study of language.* London, UK: Pearson Education.

Fleming, D. (2003). Building personal and nation-state identities: Research and practice. *TESL Canada Journal, 20*(2), 65–79.

Fleras, A., & Elliott, J. L. (2002). *Engaging diversity: Multiculturalism in Canada* (2nd ed.). Toronto, ON: Nelson Thomson Learning.

Fraser, N. (2009). *Scales of justice: Reimagining political space in a globalizing world.* New York, NY: Columbia University Press.

Gibb, T. (2008). Bridging Canadian adult second language education and essential skills policies: Approach with caution. *Adult Education Quarterly, 58*(4), 318–334.

Giles, W. (1988). Language rights are women's rights: Discrimination against immigrant women in Canadian language training policies. *Resources for Feminist Research, 17*(3), 129–132.

Guo, S. (2009). Difference, deficiency, devaluation: Tracing the roots of non-recognition of foreign credentials for immigrant professionals in Canada. *The Canadian Journal for the Study of Adult Education, 22*(1), 37–52.

Guo, S. (2010). Toward recognitive justice: Emerging trends and challenges in transnational migration and lifelong learning. *International Journal of Lifelong Education, 29*(2), 149–167.

Guo, S. (2013). Economic integration of recent Chinese immigrants in Canada's second-tier cities: The triple glass effect and immigrants' downward social mobility. *Canadian Ethnic Studies, 45*(3), 95–115.

Guo, Y. (2009). Racializing immigrant professionals in an employment preparation ESL program. *Cultural and Pedagogical Inquiry, 1*(1), 40–54.

Haque, E. (2012). *Multiculturalism within a bilingual framework: Language, race, and belonging.* Toronto, ON: University of Toronto Press.

Hunt, A. (1999). *Governing morals: A social history of moral regulation.* Cambridge, UK: Cambridge University.

Illieva, R. (2000). Exploring culture in texts designed for use in adult ESL classrooms. *TESL Canada Journal, 17*(2), 50–63.

James, C. E., & Burnaby, B. (2003). Immigrant students and schooling in Toronto, 1960s to 1990s. In P. Anisef & M. Lanphier (Eds.), *The world in a city* (pp. 263–315). Toronto, ON: University of Toronto Press.

Joshee, R. (1996). The federal government and citizenship education for newcomers. *Canadian and International Education, 25*, 108–127.

Kincheloe, J. L., & Steinberg, S. R. (1997). *Changing multiculturalism.* Buckingham, UK: Open University.

Li, P. S. (2003a). *Destination Canada: Immigration debates and issues.* Don Mills, ON: Oxford University Press.

Li, P. S. (2003b). Deconstructing Canada's discourse of immigrant integration. *Journal of International Migration and Integration, 4*(3), 315–333.

Manpower and Immigration Canada. (1970). *Immigration and population statistics.* Ottawa, ON: Information Canada.

Manpower and Immigration Canada. (1974). *The immigration program.* Ottawa, ON: Information Canada.

McDonald, L., George, U., Cleghorn, L., & Karenova, K. (2008). *An analysis of second language training programs for older adults across Canada.* Toronto, ON: University of Toronto.

Mercer, J. (1995). Canadian cities and their immigrants: New realities. *Annals of the American Academy of Political and Social Science, 538*, 169–184.

Munro, M. (2003). A primer on accent discrimination in the Canadian context. *TESL Canada Journal, 20*(2), 38–51.

Ng, R., & Shan, H. (2010). Lifelong learning as ideological practice: An analysis from the perspective of immigrant women in Canada. *International Journal of Lifelong Education, 29*(2), 169–184.

Reitz, J. G. (2005). Tapping immigrants' skills: New directions for Canadian immigration policy in the knowledge economy. *Institute for Research on Public Policy (IRPP) Choice*, *11*(1), 1–18. Retrieved from http://irpp.org/research-studies/choices-vol11-no1/

Satzewich, V., & Liodakis, N. (2007). *Race and ethnicity in Canada: A critical introduction*. Don Mills, ON: Oxford University Press.

Sauvè, V. (1996). Working with the cultures of Canada in the ESL classroom: A response to Robert Courchêne. *TESL Canada Journal, 13*(2), 17–23.

Soveran, L. (2011). *Empowerment and conformity: An ethnography of a bridge-to-work program for immigrant women* (Unpublished master's thesis). University of Calgary, Calgary, Alberta, Canada.

Statistics Canada. (2013). *Immigration and ethnocultural diversity.* Retrieved from http://www12.statcan.gc.ca/nhs-enm/video/video-eto-eng.cfm

Walsh, J. (2008). Navigating globalization: Immigration policy in Canada and Australia, 1945–2007. *Sociological Forum, 23*(4), 786–813.

Waterhouse, M. (2011). Deleuzian experimentations in Canadian immigrant language education: Research, practice, and policy. *Policy Futures in Education, 9*(4), 505–517.

YAN GUO is an associate professor in Language and Diversity at the Werklund School of Education, the University of Calgary, Canada.

This chapter describes international policy contexts of adult literacy and language assessment and the shift toward standardization through measurement tools. It considers the implications the quantification of learning outcomes has for pedagogy and practice and for the social inclusion of transnational migrants.

Literacy and Language Education: The Quantification of Learning

Tara Gibb

[Employers] were very results oriented and wanted to see real tangible proof. Like, 'can you give them another test and tell me how much better they do on the test,' that kind of thing. Difficult to demonstrate and I think some of benefits [of the language program] in the long run were less tangible, things like increased confidence and immigrant professionals self-reporting that they spoke up more in meetings. (Community college language practitioner)

Regimes of testing and benchmarking have become commonplace in adult literacy and language education. In an age of transnational migration, recent cohorts of immigrants tend to be better educated than citizens of the host nations and previous generations of immigrants across many regions of the globe (Kahanec, Kim, & Zimmerman, 2013; Reitz, 2001). Newcomers, however, experience unemployment or underemployment, and deficient literacy and language proficiency is cited as one cause (Chiswick & Miller, 2013). The policy response has been to develop national and international literacy and language assessment tools. These regimes are not isolated to literacy and language education but exist within a global discourse of standardization in skills assessment, promoted through research and policy agendas of agencies such as the Organisation for Economic Co-operation and Development (Grek, 2013).

For nations that rely on immigration to participate in the so-called global knowledge economy, the theoretical approaches, expectations, and values underpinning these tools and tests are debated among policymakers, professional regulatory bodies, employers, researchers, and practitioners. Meanwhile, the integration of immigrants and refugees into a new country involves exposure to tests and more tests, and entry into employment is dependent on

New Directions for Adult and Continuing Education, no. 146, Summer 2015 © 2015 Wiley Periodicals, Inc.
Published online in Wiley Online Library (wileyonlinelibrary.com) • DOI: 10.1002/ace.20131

achieving a predetermined level of competence. Success on these tests, however, still does not guarantee employment in stable and secure occupations that are commensurate with one's level of education and work experience.

Following, I present a survey of the literature on the policy response where literacy and language are constructed as acquisitive skills measured according to national frameworks and international tests. The chapter addresses the policy context in which the assessment regimes are situated by drawing on examples from Anglo-American countries such as Australia, Canada, New Zealand, Scotland, the United Kingdom, and the United States. Developments in ethnographic research and practice theory are also discussed, focusing on the implications the quantification of literacy and language education has for programming, pedagogy, and social inclusion.

The Policy Context

The knowledge economy has become an influential set of discourses where stiff competition exists in a global war for talent as companies and governments compete to attract the best and the brightest through a transnationally mobile labor force (Brown & Tannock, 2009). Embedded in knowledge economy discourses is an assumption that highly skilled and educated mobile knowledge workers will be employed in text-saturated environments where they will be expected to demonstrate sophisticated manipulation of signs and symbols (Farrell, 2006; Luke, 1996). Lesley Farrell (2001) has explained that the new work order is also a *new word order*, and Monica Heller (2013) has commented that the workforce has transformed into a *wordforce*. Workers are expected to document work practices, engage with information and communication technologies, demonstrate communicative competence, and produce standardized texts.

Since the 1980s, the programming of local and national education initiatives has become increasingly informed by international and supranational organizations such as the Organisation for Economic Co-operation and Development (OECD) (Rubenson, 2008). Although mainly an economic organization, the OECD has become one of several key actors (other examples include the World Bank) in educational governance globally through the proliferation of performance measures and international comparative testing (Grek, 2013; Rizvi & Lingard, 2010). Tests and numerical representation of competence give the appearance of objectivity, legitimacy, and truth (Shohamy, 2001).

Under these conditions, the literacy and language competence of immigrants are perceived as so important that national governments have placed more emphasis on the demonstration of these competencies as a requirement prior to migration (Boyd & Cao, 2009). Literacy and language education have become increasingly regulated and controlled through the development of international tests, national assessment frameworks, and established credentials for literacy and language educators (Hamilton & Barton, 2000; Hamilton & Pitt, 2011). Education systems, including adult literacy and language education, are being governed by a discourse of numbers, skills, and competence (Grek, 2009). The policy discourses regulating literacy and language education have been informed by instrumental and functional approaches, shifting literacy and language education from a humanistic community-based practice to a centralized, standardized, and managerial enterprise intended to meet the demands of the market (Bowl, 2014; Darville, 2002; Hamilton & Tett, 2012). The assumption is that immigrants who demonstrate strong literacy and language skills will integrate more smoothly into the host nation, pose less of a drain on national resources, and require fewer programs and services.

The burgeoning development and use of national and international assessment frameworks and tests is a means of regulating transnational migrant labor. Some scholars argue that these assessment frameworks position literacy and language competence as gatekeeping or boundary phenomena despite the opening of borders for economic and trade-related reasons (Baba & Dahl-Jørgensen, 2013; Hunter, 2012; Warriner, 2007). The assessment of literacy and language through standardized tests and benchmarking frameworks is one means governments and organizations employ to regulate transnational migration flows and results assist in deciding who might or might not be suitable candidates for immigration.

Theorizing and Research in Literacy and Language

In an age of globalization, knowledge work, and transnational migration, scholars argue that a focus on standardization through the development of universal measurement tools is problematic. Counter to the policy response, New Literacy Studies (NLS) employs ethnographic approaches and social practice theories to inform research into understanding literacies as multiple and varied practices situated in everyday cultural knowledge and action (Jackson, 2004; Street, 2012). Similarly, theories and research on languages in applied linguistics and sociolinguistics are challenging modernist constructions of languages as fixed systems composed of discrete skills such as listening, reading, writing, and speaking that can be measured independently of one another (Blommaert, 2010; Pennycook, 2007). As Barton (2001) has observed, disciplinary constructions have placed a border between written and spoken language, but in an increasingly textually mediated world, ethnographic research demonstrates a complex relationship between written texts and spoken language.

Although NLS is no longer new (Gee, 2012), recent developments in theories of languages as practices, multimodalities, and social semiotics offer recognition for the range of meaning-making practices in which people engage, further informing the ways that "reading and writing and their associated signs vary across cultural time and space" (Street, 2012, p. 25). Languages are often viewed as unaffected by globalization, but in fact globalization is destabilizing traditional conceptions of languages as fixed systems tied to national identities (Blommaert, 2010). The same can be said for literacies. As people move across regions and between nation–states for employment or to seek refuge, they speak variations of their first and additional languages while simultaneously engaging in an array of literacy practices, informed by their experiences and location in particular sociocultural relations. The convergence of research in literacy and language education, informed by ethnographic methods and practice theories, is leading to an understanding of how literacies and languages are aspects of social activity and generated from the cultural landscape of particular localities, giving recognition to the variation that exists in social practices (Canagarajah, 2008; Pennycook, 2010; Street, 2012).

These developments have significant implications for the assessment of immigrants' and refugees' literacy and language abilities. They offer recognition for the ways that literacy and language education is a cultural, political, and ideological construct (Gee, 2012; Street, 2012). As Street (2011) has argued, employing social practice theories and ethnographic approaches to literacies and understanding them as multiple and culturally varied practices avoid "simplistic and often ethnocentric claims regarding the consequences of literacy based on one-dimensional and culturally narrow categories and definitions" and they "can sensitize us to the ways in which the power to name and define is a crucial component of inequality" (Street, 2011, p. 580). Social practice theories acknowledge that literacies and languages are not acquisitive, culturally neutral technical skills, but that they are varied situated ways of sociocultural knowing. These developments offer insights that could inform assessment practices that acknowledge and legitimate literacy and language practices generated from different knowledge cultures.

Quantifying Literacy and Language Education: Implications

Despite the research and theoretical developments that have expanded conceptions of literacies and languages, the dominant policy response has been to develop universal and standardized assessment frameworks and tests. As Atkinson (2012) has commented, the fact that policies on assessment do not build on the substantial body of knowledge found in literacy practice is a point of frustration for advocates and practitioners. In the following section, I cite examples of literacy and language tests and frameworks before drawing on some of the literacies and languages literature from Anglo-American studies to discuss the implications that current assessment regimes have on the programming, pedagogy, and social inclusion of immigrants.

Tests and Frameworks. National literacy policy in many countries has been informed by three literacy surveys: the OECD-supported International Adult Literacy Survey (IALS), a standardized assessment of literacy and numeracy modeled after the American developed National Adult Literacy Survey (Reder & Bynner, 2009); the Adult Literacy and Lifeskills Survey (ALL); and the OECD Program for the International Assessment of Adult Competencies (PIAAC). These surveys have been developed to establish international comparisons of adult literacy and skills, to link literacy with other economic and social indicators such as wealth and health, and to inform policy through consensus (Grek, 2013; Hamilton & Barton, 2000).

In the case of language assessment, the Cambridge ESOL International English Language Testing System (IELTS) and the Test of English as a Foreign Language (TOEFL) are used by postsecondary institutions and professional regulatory bodies to determine candidates' language competence for entry into university programs or professional practice. They are also used by some national governments in such countries as the United Kingdom, New Zealand, and Canada to establish whether applicants are suitable candidates for immigration.

At the national and regional level, governments have also developed competency frameworks and measurement scales designed to standardize literacy and language teaching and assessment practices. Some examples include *Skills for Life* in the United Kingdom, the *Common European Framework of Reference for Language* (CEFR), *Svenska för invandrare* in Sweden, the *Certificate in Spoken and Written English* (CSWE) in Australia, and the *Canadian Language Benchmarks* in Canada. These frameworks attempt to integrate curriculum, pedagogy, and assessment to improve people's mobility through the provision of portable credentials that can be recognized across institutions (Little, 2011; North, 2014; Pawlikowska-Smith, 2005; Sandwall, 2010). Even though not all of these tests and frameworks are directly funded or supported by the OECD, they all reflect the burgeoning assessment regime of adult literacy and language education. The similarity between national and regional responses is not a coincidence; it reflects how policy travels under globalization through the expertise found in transnational networks of social actors (Grek, 2013; Rubenson, 2008).

Programming and Pedagogy. Regimes of testing and assessment have several implications for pedagogy and practice. One is a shift in adult literacy and language programming from a focus on civic and social participation to one of labor market attachment. Hamilton and Pitt (2011) have documented this shift in their detailed and comparative analysis of the United Kingdom's 1970s literacy policy *A Right to Read* with New Labor's 2001 release of the *Skills for Life* Strategy document. They found that discourses in England had shifted from literacy as a right for civic participation to poor literacy skills as an individual deficit that required remediation for entry into the existing economic order. They noted that literacy was no longer viewed as means for social transformation in the vein of literacy educator Paulo Freire, but that the *Skills for Life* document is framed by a neoliberal discourse where literacy is equated with employability and earnings.

In the Canadian context, Pinsent-Johnson (2014) has documented how international literacy testing has been situated in employability and skills discourses through the federal government's *Essential Skills* strategy. She has commented that the "literacy-for-competitiveness-and-productivity" discourse is not new but is intensified through policies that link the outcomes of literacy programming with employability. In my research, also situated in Canada, I documented how language practitioners negotiated employers' expectations that language assessment frameworks and tests would ease complex employment relations (Gibb, 2012). Even in countries such as Scotland, which has had a strong commitment to social practices and justice historically, Tett (2014) has noted that it is increasingly difficult for educators to resist global discourses of financial accountability that link education to employability. These testing and assessment frameworks send a strong message to immigrants and refugees that belonging and participating in their adopted home is based on their labor market attachment.

A second observation cited in the literature is that the assessment tools and frameworks are in themselves problematic. Hamilton and Barton (2000) analyzed the IALS from a literacy practices perspective, arguing that the test paints only a partial picture of literacy despite policy claims that it represents all aspects of literacy. In particular, their analysis demonstrated how attempts to remove all cultural bias from test items to ensure validity across cultures resulted in testing items bearing no reflection of what people actually do with literacy in their day-to-day lives. In a similar vein, Haque and Cray (2006) have argued that the *Canadian Language Benchmarks* do not reflect how Canadians actually engage with the English language and only prepares learners with basic proficiency. They asserted that the framework takes a deficit approach to language learning and learners are positioned as passive and accommodating recipients of language instruction. In the case of the CEFR, it is intended to promote practitioner and learner reflection but has nonetheless become a metric for testing and assessment (Jones & Saville, 2009; Little, 2011; Sandwall, 2010). Brindley (2000) has commented that it is difficult to produce reliable and high-quality information based on universal assessment frameworks unless governments and policymakers maintain a sustained commitment to the professional development of assessors and instructors.

The literature illustrates that these tests and frameworks are often based on abstract and instrumental constructions of literacies and languages. Rather than fostering understandings of what people actually do in their literacy and language practices, these assessments present idealized forms (Atkinson, 2012). Furthermore, language and literacy practices are constructed as culturally neutral, giving little recognition to the ways that practices are socially and locally situated. It is unlikely that assessments focused on universal standardization are offering accurate depictions of immigrants' and refugees' communicative competence. Furthermore, assessment from a perspective of deficit obscures immigrants' existing knowledge and skill.

A third implication observed in the literature is that adult literacy and language educators are subject to increased amounts of reporting expected to demonstrate instructor and program accountability. In her analysis of Australia's Language, Literacy, and Numeracy Program (LLNP), Ollerhead's (2010) research participants found themselves drowning in paperwork as they tried to meet the demands of an expanding bureaucratic system. In a comparative study of literacy and language educators in England and New Zealand, the participants in Bowl's (2014) study encountered philosophical tensions between their social justice perspectives of education and the demand to meet the instrumental and prescribed program outcomes. Discussing the United States' Adult Education and Family Literacy Act (AEFLA), Rose (2009) noted the U.S. Department of Education's plan to ensure accountability through a system in which states will be rewarded by meeting and exceeding performance targets. Those providers deemed less successful will be given models and methods to improve their ability to meet performance outcomes (Rose, 2009).

Although several of the studies cited here noted the ways that adult educators engaged in what Bowl (2014) has termed *microresistances* to expanding regulation, their practices are restricted by limited and narrow conceptions of literacy and language. Although the quantification of learning is expected to ensure programs and educators are accountable, these frameworks have been found to increase focus on relating classroom-based activities to meet the outcomes of the framework at the expense of the sociocultural information immigrants and refugees require for living in a new country (Burns, 1996; Haque & Cray, 2006).

Social Inclusion and Adult Education. What do these systems of measurement scales, tests, and benchmarks mean for social inclusion? Rather than fostering economic and social integration, these assessment tools construct a limited understanding of the knowledge that immigrants and refugees embody. They construct universal or national understandings of literacy and language when in fact only certain forms of literacies and standard versions of languages are privileged in the tests and frameworks (Hamilton, 2001; Pennycook, 2001). The appeal for standardized assessment frameworks leaves little space for pluralistic ways of knowing and denies the centrality of culture, social relations, and locality in people's daily literacy and language practices. Culture is treated as an error (Hamilton & Barton, 2000), whereas difference is perceived as deficit (Street, 2011). Literacies and languages are situated in social environments and intertwined with the social and power relations of particular locations (Hunter, 2004; Pennycook, 2010).

It is difficult, however, to give recognition to different ways of naming literacies (Street, 2011) and variations of language in assessment systems that attempt to standardize knowledge. Under such testing systems, immigrants and refugees are classified and measured according to dominant conceptions of what constitutes literacy and language proficiency. Newcomers are viewed as in deficit, needing to upskill to be deemed employable. Furthermore, as Pinsent-Johnson (2014) has demonstrated, testing and assessment frameworks have led to a reduction in programming in some cases, particularly for groups of learners who are not deemed economically efficient. Standardized and universal approaches to assessment and practice maintain cultural hierarchies and perpetuate social and economic stratification (Maddox, Aikman, Rao, & Robinson-Pant, 2011).

For immigrants and refugees who do transition to the workplace, responsibility for learning to communicate across cultural codes is often placed on newcomers (Gibb, 2012), and the collaborative work people engage in while participating in literacy and language practices (Blommaert, 2010) is not acknowledged. Standardized assessment frameworks currently assess individual literacy and language practices. Assessment practices that included representations of how immigrants communicate while working collectively could offer more accurate understandings of competence.

Existing testing regimes, therefore, do not bode well for the social inclusion of immigrants and refugees. Maddox et al. (2011) have commented that ethnographic approaches and practice theories are advancing the recognition of values, context, and plurality but that dialogue with policy actors requires strengthening. Immigrants and refugees arrive in host nations with literacy and language practices that might be different but nonetheless legitimate. As the passage at the beginning of the chapter illustrates, discourses on tests obscure other valuable outcomes of learning, which policy actors and employers overlook. Facilitating dialogue, therefore, could include inviting policymakers and employers into literacy and language classrooms so that they might observe firsthand alternative forms of assessment, view holistic representations of language and literacy practices, and listen to immigrants' experiences and expressions of knowledge. Meanwhile, policymakers could be more open to participatory policymaking where practitioners, researchers, and immigrants are invited to inform policy. Recognition for how literacies and languages are situated in and informed by different cultural and social relations offers a more expansive understanding for the social inclusion of immigrants and refugees.

References

Atkinson, T. (2012). Beyond disempowering counts: Mapping a fruitful future for adult literacies. In L. Tett, M. Hamilton, & J. Crowther (Eds.), *More powerful literacies* (pp. 75–87). Leicester, United Kingdom: NIACE.

Baba, M. L., & Dahl-Jørgensen, C. (2013). Language policy in practice: Re-bordering the nation. *International Migration, 51*(2), 60–76. doi:10.1111/imig.12048

Barton, D. (2001). Directions for literacy research: Analysing language and social practices in a textually mediated world. *Language and Education, 15*(2–3), 92–104. doi:10.1080/09500780108666803

Blommaert, J. (2010). *The sociolinguistics of globalization.* New York, NY: Cambridge University Press.

Bowl, M. (2014). "Ducking and diving" adult educator agency in testing times: Insights from England and New Zealand. *Globalisation, Societies and Education, 12*(1), 32–50.

Boyd, M., & Cao, X. (2009). Immigrant language proficiency, earnings, and language policies. *Canadian Studies in Population, 36*(1–2), 63–86.

Brindley, G. (2000). Assessment in the Adult Migrant English Program. In G. Brindley (Ed.), *Studies in immigrant English language assessment* (Vol. 1, pp. 1–43). Sydney, NSW: Macquarie University.

Brown, P., & Tannock, S. (2009). Education, meritocracy and the global war for talent. *Journal of Education Policy, 24*(4), 377–392.

Burns, A. (1996). Collaborative research and curriculum change in the Australian Adult Migrant English Program. *TESOL Quarterly*, *30*(3), 591–598.

Canagarajah, A. S. (2008). Reconstructing local knowledge, reconfiguring language studies. In A. S. Canagarajah (Ed.), *Reclaiming the local in language policy and practice* (pp. 3–24). New York, NY: Routledge.

Chiswick, B. R., & Miller, P. W. (2013). The impact of surplus skills on earnings: Extending the over-education model to language proficiency. *Economics of Education Review*, *36*, 253–275. doi:10.1016/j.econedurev.2013.07.008

Darville, R. (2002). *Policy, accountability and practice in adult literacy work: Sketching an institutional ethnography*. Paper presented at the 21st annual conference of the Canadian Association for the Study of Adult Education, Ontario Institute for Studies in Education, University of Toronto, Toronto, Canada. Retrieved from http://www.casae-aceea.ca /sites/casae/archives/cnf2002/2002_Papers/darville2002w.pdf

Farrell, L. (2001). The "new word order": Workplace education and the textual practice of economic globalization. *Pedagogy, Culture and Society*, *9*(1), 57–75. doi:10.1080 /14681360100200103

Farrell, L. (2006). *Making knowledge common: Literacy and knowledge at work*. New York, NY: Peter Lang.

Gee, J. P. (2012). *Social linguistics and literacies: Ideology in discourses* (4th ed.). New York, NY: Routledge.

Gibb, T. L. (2012). *Knowledge economy discourses and language regulation: An analysis of policy processes in adult English language education in Canada* (Unpublished doctoral dissertation). The University of British Columbia, Vancouver, BC.

Grek, S. (2009). Governing by numbers: The PISA "effect" in Europe. *Journal of Education Policy*, *24*(1), 23–37. doi:10.1080/02680930802412669

Grek, S. (2013). Expert moves: International comparative testing and the rise of expertocracy. *Journal of Education Policy*, *28*(5), 695–709.

Hamilton, M. (2001). Privileged literacies: Policy, institutional process and the life of the IALS. *Language and Education*, *15*(2–3), 178–196.

Hamilton, M., & Barton, D. (2000). The International Adult Literacy Survey: What does it really measure? *International Review of Education*, *46*(5), 377–389.

Hamilton, M., & Pitt, K. (2011). Changing policy discourses: Constructing literacy inequalities. *International Journal of Educational Development*, *31*, 596–605. doi:10.1016/j .ijedudev.2011.02.011

Hamilton, M., & Tett, L. (2012). More powerful literacies: The policy context. In L. Tett, M. Hamilton, & J. Crowther (Eds.), *More powerful literacies* (pp. 31–57). Leicester, UK: NIACE.

Haque, E., & Cray, E. (2006). Putting them in their place: Language policies and newcomers to Canada. In N. Amin & G. J. S. Dei (Eds.), *The poetics of anti-racism* (pp. 73–84). Halifax, NS: Fernwood.

Heller, M. (2013). Language as resource in the globalized economy. In N. Coupland (Ed.), *The handbook of language and globalization* (pp. 349–365). Chichester, West Sussex, UK: Wiley-Blackwell.

Hunter, J. (2004). Implications for theory. In M. E. Belfiore, T. A. Defoe, S. Folinsbee, J. Hunter, & N. S. Jackson (Eds.), *Reading work: Literacies in the new workplace* (pp. 241–260). Mahwah, NJ: Lawrence Erlbaum Associates.

Hunter, J. (2012). Transnational migrants in the workplace: Agency and opportunity. In L. Tett, M. Hamilton, & J. Crowther (Eds.), *More powerful literacies* (pp. 165–178). Leicester, United Kingdom: NIACE.

Jackson, N. (2004). Introduction: Reading work. In M. E. Belfiore, T. A. Defoe, S. Folinsbee, J. Hunter, & N. S. Jackson (Eds.), *Reading work: Literacies in the new workplace* (pp. 1–15). Mahwah, NJ: Lawrence Erlbaum.

Jones, N., & Saville, N. (2009). European language policy: Assessment, learning, and the CEFR. *Annual Review of Applied Linguistics, 29*, 51–63. doi:10.1017/S02671905 09090059

Kahanec, M., Kim, A. M.-H., & Zimmerman, K. F. (2013). Pitfalls of immigration inclusion into the European welfare state. *International Journal of Manpower, 34*(1), 39–55. doi:10.1108/01437721311319647

Little, D. (2011). The Common European Framework of Reference for Languages: A research agenda. *Language Teaching, 44*(3), 381–393. doi:10.1017/S0261444811000097

Luke, A. (1996). Text and discourse in education: An introduction to critical discourse analysis. *Review of Research in Education, 21*, 3–48.

Maddox, B., Aikman, S., Rao, N., & Robinson-Pant, A. (2011). Literacy inequalities and social justice. *International Journal of Educational Development, 31*, 577–579. doi:10.1016/j.ijedudev.2011.04.003

North, B. (2014). Putting the Common European Framework of Reference to good use. *Language Teaching, 47*(2), 228–249. doi:10.1017/S0261444811000206

Ollerhead, S. (2010). Teacher agency and policy response in the adult ESL literacy classroom. *TESOL Quarterly, 44*(3), 606–618. doi:10.5054/tq.2010.230742_1

Pawlikowska-Smith, G. (2005). *Canadian language benchmarks 2000: English as a second language for adults.* Ottawa, ON: Citizenship and Immigration Canada.

Pennycook, A. (2001). *Critical applied linguistics: A critical introduction.* Mahwah, NJ: Lawrence Erlbaum Associates.

Pennycook, A. (2007). *Global Englishes and transcultural flows.* New York, NY: Routledge.

Pennycook, A. (2010). *Language as a local practice.* New York, NY: Routledge.

Pinsent-Johnson, C. (2014, May). *The coordination of adult literacy policy and pedagogy to ensure productivity in a knowledge economy.* Paper presented at the annual conference of the Canadian Association for the Study of Adult Education, Brock University, St. Catherines, Canada.

Reder, S., & Bynner, J. (2009). Introduction: The need for longitudinal studies in adult literacy and numeracy education. In S. Reder & J. Bynner (Eds.), *Tracking adult literacy and numeracy skills: Findings from longitudinal research* (pp. 1–23). New York, NY: Routledge.

Reitz, J. G. (2001). Immigrant success in the knowledge economy: Institutional change and the immigrant experience, 1970–1995. *Journal of Social Issues, 57*(3), 579–613.

Rizvi, F., & Lingard, B. (2010). *Globalizing education policy.* New York, NY: Routledge.

Rose, S. (2009). Using a longitudinal approach with state administrative records to evaluate adult education programs in the United States. In S. Reder & J. Bynner (Eds.), *Tracking adult literacy and numeracy skills: Findings from longitudinal research* (pp. 281–295). New York, NY: Routledge.

Rubenson, K. (2008). OECD education policies and world hegemony. In R. Mahon & S. McBride (Eds.), *OECD and transnational governance* (pp. 242–259). Vancouver, BC: UBC Press.

Sandwall, K. (2010). "I learn more at school": A critical perspective on workplace-related second language learning in and out of school. *TESOL Quarterly, 44*(3), 542–574. doi:10.5054/tq.2010.229270

Shohamy, E. (2001). *The power of tests: A critical perspective on the uses of language tests.* Harlow, England: Pearson Education Limited.

Street, B. (2011). Literacy inequalities in theory and practice: The power to name and define. *International Journal of Educational Development, 31*, 580–586. doi:10.1016/j.ijedudev.2010.09.005

Street, B. (2012). Contexts for literacy work: New Literacy Studies, multimodality, and the "local and the global." In L. Tett, M. Hamilton, & J. Crowther (Eds.), *More powerful literacies* (pp. 15–30). Leicester, UK: NIACE.

Tett, L. (2014). Comparative performance measures, globalising strategies and literacy policy in Scotland. *Globalisation, Societies and Education*, *12*(1), 127–142. doi:10.1080 /14767724.2013.858996

Warriner, D. S. (2007). "It's just the nature of the beast": Re-imagining the literacies of schooling in adult ESL education. *Linguistics and Education*, *18*, 305–324.

TARA GIBB is currently a Social Sciences and Humanities Research Council of Canada postdoctoral fellow at the Werklund School of Education, University of Calgary, Canada.

Drawing on practice-based learning theory, this chapter examines issues pertaining to the deskilling of immigrant professionals in Canada. It argues that adult educators need to have an awareness of transnational migration dynamics and work in meaningful ways to keep immigrant professionals connected to professional knowledge practices.

Migrating Professional Knowledge: Progressions, Regressions, and Dislocations

Bonnie L. Slade

Migration, moving from one country to another, implicates professionals in multiple transitions, many of which are unexpected and unwelcomed. Since the 1990s skilled migration for permanent and temporary settlement has been rapidly increasing. In the global competition for skilled migrants, professionals are highly sought after in both traditional immigrant-receiving countries (Canada, United States, Australia) and increasingly in more historically restrictive regions, such as the European Union. For national governments of immigrant-receiving countries, professional migration is viewed as strategic, addressing labor market shortages, as well as dealing with issues of aging populations and low birth rates. Aspects of migration such as population flows, settlement, and integration are well researched and are generally approached from an economic, demographic, sociological, or cultural perspective. From an adult education perspective, researchers examine how professional knowledge crosses national borders, encountering new systems of professional regulation and higher education, facing different value systems related to professional knowledge and experience, new gender configurations of professions, different work practices and material realities.

Although migration is a very contentious issue, research has shown that both policymakers and citizens believe that skilled migration is beneficial to the economy, culture, and professional practices of a country (Park, Clery, Curtice, Phillips, & Utting, 2012, p. 36). The perceived benefit of professional migration, however, rests on certain assumptions about the labor market integration of these professionals. Critically, it assumes that they will be able to practice their profession, providing essential services and contributing to the growth of the economy. Adult educators in Canada have shown that the economic promise of skilled migration is often not realized. Many professionals

NEW DIRECTIONS FOR ADULT AND CONTINUING EDUCATION, no. 146, Summer 2015 © 2015 Wiley Periodicals, Inc.
Published online in Wiley Online Library (wileyonlinelibrary.com) • DOI: 10.1002/ace.20132

experience difficulties in establishing themselves in professional practice in Canada, facing deskilling and labor market exclusion. Although Canada purposefully recruits a high numbers of skilled workers annually, migration to Canada for professionals has been shown to be a risky endeavor.

Drawing on three empirical research projects as well as related literature on transnational migration and adult education, this paper examines the professional trajectory of immigrants in Canada, arguing that deskilling is itself a transition that can be empirically investigated through examining the knowledge practices of immigrant professionals. Current approaches to understanding workplace learning stress that professional knowledge cannot be separated from work practices. Researchers from education, organizational studies, and science and technology studies assert that knowing itself is a practical activity enmeshed in the social and material relations of work (Bruni, Gherardi, & Parolin, 2007; Fenwick & Edwards, 2010; Lave & Wenger, 1991; Orlikowski, 2002; Schatzki, 2001). These ideas have profound implications for understanding workplace learning and professional knowledge, but they have not been applied to the migration of professionals across national borders. This chapter raises questions about how deskilling is accomplished through exclusions and inclusions in various knowledge practices.

This paper is presented in four sections. First, I outline the background of Canadian immigration policy, and the research on the labor market outcomes of immigrant professionals in Canada. In the second section I detail the research on deskilling, drawing on three qualitative research studies in particular (Mirchandani et al., 2010; Slade, 2011; Slade & Schugurensky, 2010). The next section details the labor market exclusion of immigrants, either through unemployment or working without pay. The final section draws out some thoughts on migration and professional transitions and implications for adult education policy and practice.

Background—Canadian Immigration Policy

The explicit goal of Canadian immigration policy is to attract the "best and the brightest" for both permanent and, increasingly also temporary, migration (Kenney, 2012). The result of Canada's robust immigration strategy with its stringent selection process has been the creation of a large pool of professionals with international credentials and work experience, many of whom are unemployed or underemployed (Gogia & Slade, 2011). Research indicates that immigrants' education and work experience is consistently undervalued in Canada, resulting in higher levels of unemployment, lower earnings, and deskilling for individual immigrants and their families (Creese & Wiebe, 2009; Grenier & Xue, 2011; Li, 2005; Preston et al., 2010; Reitz, 2007; Slade, 2011, 2012). In relation to national productivity, studies have estimated that the lack of recognition of skilled immigrants' credentials and prior learning has a negative impact on Canadian economic performance by approximately $15 billion annually (Reitz, 2001). The links between immigration status, unemployment, poverty, and racial origin have been investigated, and it has been argued that there exists a racialized and gendered labor market where people of color, particularly women, are overrepresented in low-income sectors (Guo, 2009, 2010; Mirchandani et al., 2010; Ng, 1996; Shan, 2009, 2012; Xu, 2012).

A wide range of barriers have been identified by researchers, government task forces, community advocacy groups, and immigrants themselves: credential assessment and recognition processes that are lengthy and individualized, devaluation of international work experience, limited opportunities to gain relevant appropriate Canadian work experience, discrimination, lack of professional networks, difficulties adapting to Canadian culture, lack of knowledge of Canadian standards and practices, cumbersome and costly licensing processes, language issues, and employers' lack of knowledge about international systems. According to the Longitudinal Survey of Immigrants to Canada (LSIC), although 76% of new immigrants have at least one type of international credential, such as a university degree, 70% experienced barriers in gaining access to the Canadian labor market at an appropriate level. The biggest barrier to finding appropriate employment for immigrant professionals was the lack of "Canadian work experience" (Statistics Canada, 2003). LSIC also revealed that immigrants experience "occupational skidding" (Kofman, 1999, p. 283) as 6 out of 10 immigrants who were employed at the time of the survey were not working in the profession or occupation in which they were educated and experienced (Statistics Canada, 2003). The barriers are especially profound for immigrants in professions that are regulated in Canada, such as engineering (Dang, 2005; Slade, 2004).

Deskilling is a term that initially referred to the skill degradation of workers with the introduction of new technologies into the labor process (Braverman, 1974). Deskilling and the related terms *deprofessionalization* and *underemployment* have been taken up in current adult education debates to describe the experiences of immigrant professionals who end up working in their own fields but at much lower levels (and pay) than they are qualified, as well as in unrelated survival jobs characterized by low pay and irregular hours (Gibb & Hamdon, 2010; Guo, 2009, 2010; Man, 2010; Mirchandani et al., 2008, 2010; Mojab, 2000; Ng, 1996; Sakamoto, Chin, & Young, 2010; Walsh, Brigham, & Wang, 2011). For immigrants, having a non-Canadian university degree does not necessarily translate into the same financial or professional opportunities of Canadian-educated graduates. Preston et al. (2010) have shown, drawing on data from the 2006 Canadian Census, that immigrants with at least one university degree have lower annual earnings and double the unemployment rate than Canadian-born people with the same education. The discrepancy is worsening for new immigrants and is especially pronounced for highly skilled immigrant women. Deskilling leads many immigrants into poverty. Evidence of this can be found in food bank usage statistics. The Daily Bread Food Bank (2012) reported that 49% of the 1,082,000 people who relied on the food bank for basic survival in 2010–2011 were immigrants, 53% of whom had been in Canada for more than 10 years. Twenty-four percent of the immigrants had a minimum of one postsecondary credential, compared to 19% of Canadian-born food bank users.

Deskilling Through Workplace Training

Findings from the Skilled in Vulnerability: Work-related Learning in the Racialized Culture of Contingency research project, funded by the Social Science Humanities Research Council in Canada, reveal much about the process of deskilling. The purpose of the research was to examine the labor market impact of transnational migration on immigrant women in Toronto (Mirchandani et al., 2008, 2010). Semistructured, in-depth interviews were conducted in five languages with 50 women working as supermarket cashiers, call center operators, and garment sewers on a part-time, seasonal, or temporary basis. Twenty-four of the women were highly skilled immigrants with university degrees from their home countries. On average they made between seven and eight dollars an hour and received no job security or benefits; 80% of the women earned less than $20,000 per year, and 36% of the women earned less than $10,000. Several participants experienced adverse health effects due to the nature of their work. Women also noted that their family lives, educational endeavors, or social and leisure activities were frequently disrupted as a result of constant and unplanned schedule changes in their paid work.

Participants reported experiencing great difficulty in obtaining professional work in Canada, facing a number of social processes, such as professional closure, accessibility of precarious jobs, gendered family dynamics, which channeled them into low-end contingent jobs. Women noted that precarious jobs in call centers and supermarkets were easily accessible and did not require credentials or Canadian experience. Participants shared that workplace training served more as a monitoring tool than as a means to develop their capacities and confidence, and the work itself undermined their autonomy and took away their discretionary power. Learning to follow scripts, to memorize product codes for fruit and vegetables, and to sew garments as quickly as possible were a long way from their former work as accountants, engineers, and teachers. For these highly skilled immigrant women, the transition into precarious work involves, first, a material shift where women learn to deal with unstable, poorly paid jobs, and second, an ideological shift where women learn to construct themselves as precarious workers. This research revealed that for many immigrant women, transnational migration is accompanied by a jarring discontinuity between past education and work, and present occupation (Sangha, Slade, Mirchandani, Maitra, & Shan, 2012).

Separated from the networks and knowledge practices of their profession, underemployed skilled immigrants experience a double jeopardy when trying to find an appropriate job in their profession. Not only do their skills become outdated in light of changes in their fields, but they also suffer a deskilling process with respect to their original capacities. Reestablishing a professional career in a timely way is critical for immigrants. The consequences are dire

New Directions for Adult and Continuing Education • DOI: 10.1002/ace

when immigrants are out of their fields for too long, as Galabuzi (2006) asserts that, "over 90% of those who fail to find work in their field in the first three years of immigration end up permanently in other services" (p. 136). Often immigrant professionals will undertake adult education to "upgrade" their skills, or they will turn to volunteering to improve their labor market situation.

Informal Learning Through Unpaid Work

When faced with high levels of unemployment and labor market dissatisfaction (Toronto Immigrant Employment Data Initiative, 2012), many immigrant professionals undertake volunteer work as a strategy to reestablish themselves in their professions. Volunteering provides a hope of gaining access to Canadian workplaces, getting exposure to "Canadian culture" and increasing their chances of finding suitable employment. Data from the National Survey of Volunteering and Giving (Hall, McKeown, & Roberts. 2001) reveal that 30% of newer immigrants indicated that their motivation for volunteering was to improve their job opportunities. Community-based agencies through school boards are points of entry through which many immigrants find volunteer work as they offer employment-related programs with a work placement (Slade, 2011). There is a wide array of stakeholders promoting volunteerism as an effective strategy for immigrants to gain Canadian work experience. Proponents include community organizations, advocacy associations, regulatory bodies, federal and provincial government departments and ministries, academics, ethnic media, and immigrants themselves. There is, however, very little evidence to support the generally held belief that volunteering works to improve the labor market position of immigrants (Schugurensky & Slade, 2008).

To draw out the tensions, mechanics, and nuances of this transition from immigrant professional to volunteer workers, I draw on empirical data from The Informal Learning of Volunteer Workers research project (Slade & Schugurensky, 2010). The purpose of the study was to explore the connections between informal learning and volunteer work among immigrants who volunteered to improve their access to the labor market. Semistructured interviews were conducted with 45 immigrant volunteers: 30 women and 15 men. Most arrived as skilled workers, and although they came from 17 different countries, almost 47% of the participants were from China. Forty-three participants (96%) had completed at least one university degree and, on average, the participants had 10 years of professional work experience prior to immigrating to Canada. Professions included medicine, engineering, business administration, teaching, psychology, and information technology. Most participants had been in Canada for 5 years or less. With respect to age, 20% of the group were under 29 years of age and 18% were older than 40 years old. Most participants (62%) were between 30 and 39 years of age. Overall, participants embodied the intended outcome of immigration policy: they were well educated, had years of work experience in a professional field, and were the right age for the labor market.

The volunteer work placements were brokered through community-based agencies (usually through an employment assistance program) or negotiated independently by the individual. The site of volunteer work included the nonprofit (82%), for-profit (16%), and public sectors (2%). Some of the volunteer placements were part of adult education programs delivered by community organizations and local school boards. The length of time for the volunteer placements varied from 2 or 3 hours per week to full-time hours for a fixed period of time, usually 3 months. Volunteer tasks varied from placement to placement—network administration, website development, looking after children, arts and crafts for kids, teaching computer software classes, setting up and maintaining computer networks, general office support, accounting, filing tax returns, language interpreting, and wrapping gifts. Some of the tasks required only general and basic skills, such as gift wrapping, whereas the others needed more professional skills and knowledge, such as computer network setup and writing computer software code.

Although 43 of the 45 participants in the study had at least one post-secondary degree and years of relevant work experience, they experienced great difficulty in securing meaningful employment after their volunteer work. Overall, if measured by obtaining meaningful paid work as a result of the volunteer placement, this research indicates that volunteering for "Canadian work experience" is not a very successful strategy. At time of the interviews, only 13% of participants were in a job that matched their skills and experience. Almost half of the participants were either unemployed (44%) or underemployed (42%). The largest group of participants ($n = 20$) were those who were unemployed after their volunteer placements. In this group of participants, there were two immigrants with backgrounds in science who volunteered at for-profit companies writing software code. There were also 19 participants who were underemployed. Examples of this include a female engineer from Columbia who was doing quality testing in a factory, a male professor working in sales, and a female psychologist working as a waitress. Of the whole sample, half of the women (50%) and slightly more than one quarter (27%) of the men were considered underemployed.

The six participants (13%) who were able to secure work matched to their education and work experience had two things in common. The first was that the work they performed in their volunteer placement was closely connected to their educational backgrounds and work experience. The second common element to their experience, related to the first, was that through their volunteer work they were able to develop meaningful social networks. For these participants, the volunteer work acted as a successful stepping stone to paid work, as it allowed them to draw on their prior professional experience from abroad while building social and cultural capital in Canada in their profession (Bourdieu, 2004). They were able to remain connected to the knowledge practices of their profession.

Although most participants reported that they had increased their confidence, self-esteem, and social and cultural capital through their volunteer placements, their experiences raise questions about volunteering as a direct transition to the labor market. For employers and the Canadian economy, however, there are measurable benefits to these poor labor market options for immigrants. It is difficult to measure the actual financial contribution of the volunteer labor of immigrant professionals. However, an analysis of one adult education program offered through local school boards in Ontario conservatively estimated that in 1 year immigrant volunteers performed over 1.92 million hours of work, the equivalent of over 923 full-time jobs, representing almost 20 million dollars of unpaid wages (Slade, 2011, 2012).

Deskilling as Exclusion From Practice: Implications for Adult Education Practice and Policy

As the experiences of immigrant professionals in Canada illustrate, transitions into professional life in a new country can involve regressions, dislocations, or progressions. This chapter has mainly detailed the experiences of professionals who are unable to smoothly navigate the various assessment and licensing processes and as a consequence are deskilled. Of course, some immigrant professionals do transition into professional work. Professionals from English-speaking countries of the British Commonwealth and from the United States who have high levels of social, cultural, and linguistic capital (Bourdieu, 2004) and are able to convincingly match their education and experience to Canadian practices have a much better chance of reestablishing their professional practice (Li, 2005). Often professional regulatory bodies will have mutual recognition agreements with other English-speaking countries, making the licensing process easier by accepting educational credentials as equivalent and removing the need for additional assessment of professional knowledge through examinations. The majority of immigrant professionals in Canada, however, are from Asia and South Asia, and issues of deskilling are particularly prevalent in these communities.

Professional regulatory bodies that are responsible for protecting the public from harm by ensuring high standards of professional practice have a challenging task to assess applications from over 100 countries against Canadian standards. Tools that they use to assess knowledge include examinations, evaluation of university transcripts, comparison of national professional regulatory systems, and references from local professionals. Researchers, community advocates, and politicians who are concerned about deskilling have raised questions about the logic and fairness of these assessments. When a medical oncologist with 15 years of professional experience migrates to Canada, how relevant is it to assess their skills and knowledge by making them take several examinations on basic medicine?

There are tensions and contradictions in the process of professional migration. The recruiting country needs the skills, energy, and international connections of professional migrants, yet, for many in Canada, the promises of a professional life often do not materialize. Professional migrants are often shocked to experience deskilling; they do not imagine migration to be a transition from professional practice to labor jobs. But although deskilling is experienced individually, it is structurally accomplished and adult education has become a vital part of the institutional response to deskilling through the provision of courses geared at helping immigrant professionals get back into their professions. Are these courses unnecessary retraining or do they provide an essential bridge back into professional work? Drawing on practice-based learning theory, it is critical to ensure immigrant professionals remain connected to the knowledge practices in their fields, whether this be through formal courses designed in partnership with professional regulatory bodies or informal communities of practice. The research illustrates how dangerous it is for immigrant professionals to be away from their professions for too long. A key component of deskilling is a profound loss of professional identity, which can be compounded by taking on a survival job or volunteering in an unrelated field. For successful labor market integration, immigrant professionals need to remain part of the knowledge practices of their profession. They cannot do this while working in a supermarket or call center or by "volunteering" in a factory (Slade, 2012).

Globally there is a tension in adult education between serving social purposes and the needs of the labor market. Adult educators need to be aware of the issues involved in transnational migration and deskilling. Critical adult educators with an awareness of these global transnational migration dynamics need to find ways to keep immigrant professionals connected to their professions and professional discourses. Employment programs without this critical structural awareness may simply be reproducing exploitation and deskilling for immigrant professionals.

References

Bourdieu, P. (2004). The forms of capital. In S. Ball (Ed.), *Reader in sociology of education* (pp. 15–29). London, UK: Routledge.

Braverman, H. (1974). *Labor and monopoly capital: The degradation of work in the twentieth century.* New York, NY: Monthly Review Press.

Bruni, A., Gherardi, S., & Parolin, L. (2007). Knowing in a system of fragmented knowledge. *Mind, Culture, and Activity, 1–2,* 83–102.

Creese, G., & Wiebe, B. (2009). "Survival employment": Gender and deskilling among African immigrants in Canada. *International Migration, 50*(5), 56–76.

Daily Bread Food Bank. (2012). *Who's hungry? Fighting hunger: 2011 profile of hunger in the GTA.* Retrieved from http://www.dailybread.ca/wp-content/uploads/2011/09/WhosHungryReport2011-WEB.pdf

Dang, M. (2005, March 27). Placement of foreign trained engineers. *The Weekender,* p. 3.

Fenwick, T., & Edwards, R. (2010). *Actor-network theory in education.* London, UK: Routledge.

Galabuzi, G. E. (2006). *Canada's economic apartheid: The social exclusion of racialized groups in the new century.* Toronto, ON: Canada's Scholars Press.

Gibb, T., & Hamdon, E. (2010). Moving across borders: Immigrant women's encounters with globalization, the knowledge economy and lifelong learning. *International Journal of Lifelong Education, 29*(2), 185–200.

Gogia, N., & Slade, B. (2011). *About Canada: Immigration.* Halifax, NS: Fernwood Publishing.

Grenier, G., & Xue, L. (2011). Canadian immigrants' access to a first job in their intended occupation. *Journal of International Migration and Integration, 12*(3), 275–303.

Guo, S. (2009). Difference, deficiency, and devaluation: Tracing the roots of non/recognition of foreign credentials for immigrant professionals in Canada. *Canadian Journal for the Study of Adult Education, 22*(1), 37–52.

Guo, S. (2010). False promises in the new economy: Barriers facing the transition of recent Chinese immigrants in Edmonton. In P. Sawchuk & A. Taylor (Eds.), *Challenging transitions in learning and work: Perspectives on policy and practice* (pp. 243–260). Rotterdam, the Netherlands: Sense Publishers.

Hall, M., McKeown, L., & Roberts, K. (2001). *Caring Canadians, involved Canadians: Highlights from the 2000 Canada survey of giving, volunteering and participating.* Ottawa, ON: Statistics Canada.

Kenney, J. (2012). *Moving towards a targeted, fast and efficient immigration system focusing on jobs, growth and prosperity.* Retrieved from http://www.cic.gc.ca/english/department /media/speeches/2012/2012-06-26.asp

Kofman, E. (1999). Female birds of passage a decade later: Gender and immigration in the European Union. *International Migration Review, 33*(2), 269–299.

Lave, J., & Wenger, E. (1991). *Situated learning: Legitimate peripheral participation.* Cambridge, UK: University of Cambridge Press.

Li, P. (2005). *Destination Canada: Immigration debates and issues.* Oxford, UK: Oxford University Press.

Man, G. (2010). Global migration, gender, and inequality: Chinese immigrant women's employment experience in Canada. In T. McCauley (Ed.), *Canadian society: Global perspectives* (pp. 129–142). Toronto, ON: De Sitter Press.

Mirchandani, K., Ng, R., Coloma-Moya, N., Maitra, S., Rawlings, T., Siddiqui, K.,... Slade, B. (2008). The paradox of training and learning in a culture of contingency. In D. Livingstone, P. Sawchuk, & K. Mirchandani (Eds.), *The future of lifelong learning and work: Critical perspectives* (pp. 171–185). Rotterdam, the Netherlands: Sense Publishers.

Mirchandani, K., Ng, R., Coloma-Moya, N., Maitra, S., Rawlings, T., Siddiqui, K.,... Slade, B. (2010). Gendered and racialized journeys into contingent work. In P. Sawchuk & A. Taylor (Eds.), *Challenging transitions in learning and work: Perspectives on policy and practice* (pp. 231–243). Rotterdam, the Netherlands: Sense Publishers.

Mojab, S. (2000). The power of economic globalization: Deskilling immigrant women through training. In R. M. Cervero, A. L. Wilson, & Associates (Eds.), *Power in practice: Adult education and the struggle for knowledge and power in society* (pp. 23–41). San Francisco, CA: Jossey-Bass.

Ng, R. (1996). *The politics of community services: Immigrant women, class and state* (2nd ed.). Halifax, NS: Fernwood Publishing.

Orlikowski, W. (2002). Knowing in practice: Enacting a collective capability in distributed organizing. *Organization Science, 13*(3), 249–273.

Park, A., Clery, E., Curtice, J., Phillips, M., & Utting, D. (Eds.). (2012). *British social attitudes: The 29th report.* London, UK: NatCen Social Research. Retrieved from www.bsa -29.natcen.ac.uk

Preston, V., Damsbaek, N., Kelly, P., Lemoine, M., Lo, L., Shields, J., & Tufts, S. (2010). *What are the labour market outcomes for university-educated immigrants?* Retrieved from http://www.yorku.ca/tiedi/doc/AnalyticalReport8.pdf

Reitz, J. G. (2001). Immigrant skill utilization in the Canadian labour market: Implications of human capital research. *Journal of International Migration and Integration*, 2(3), 347–378.

Reitz, J. G. (2007). Immigrant employment success in Canada, part II: Understanding the decline. *Journal of International Migration and Integration*, 8(1), 37–62.

Sakamoto, I., Chin, M., & Young, M. (2010). "Canadian experience," employment challenges, and skilled immigrants: A close look through "tacit knowledge." *Canadian Social Work Journal*, 10(1), 145–151.

Sangha, J., Slade, B., Mirchandani, K., Maitra, S., & Shan, H. (2012). An ethnodrama on work-related learning in precarious jobs: Racialization and resistance. *Qualitative Inquiry*, 18(3), 286–296.

Schatzki, T. (2001). Introduction: Practice theory. In T. Schatzki, K. Knorr Cetina, & E. von Savigny (Eds.), *The practice turn in contemporary theory* (pp. 1–14). London, UK: Routledge.

Schugurensky, D., & Slade, B. (2008). New immigrants, volunteer work and labour market integration: On learning and re-building social capital. In D. Livingstone, P. Sawchuk, & K. Mirchandani (Eds.), *The future of lifelong learning and work: Critical perspectives* (pp. 263–275). Rotterdam, the Netherlands: Sense Publishers.

Shan, H. (2009). Practices on the periphery: Chinese immigrant women negotiating occupational niches in Canada. *Canadian Journal for the Study of Adult Education*, 21(2), 1–18.

Shan, H. (2012). Learning to "fit in": The emotional work of Chinese immigrant engineers in Canada. *Journal of Workplace Learning*, 24(5), 351–364.

Slade, B. (2004). Highly skilled and under-theorized: Women migrant professionals. In R. B. Folson (Ed.), *Calculated kindness: Global economic restructuring and Canadian immigration & settlement policy* (pp. 102–116). Halifax, NS: Fernwood.

Slade, B. (2011). The ideological construction of "Canadian work experience": Adult education and the reproduction of labor and difference. In S. Carpenter & S. Mojab (Eds.), *Educating from Marx: Race, gender and learning* (pp. 137–166). New York, NY: Palgrave Macmillan.

Slade, B. (2012). "From high skill to high school": Illustrating the process of deskilling immigrants through reader's theatre and institutional ethnography. *Qualitative Inquiry*, 18(5), 401–413.

Slade, B., & Schugurensky, D. (2010). "Starting from another side, the bottom": Volunteer work as a transition into the labor market for immigrant professionals. In P. Sawchuk & A. Taylor (Eds.), *Challenging transitions in learning and work: Perspectives on policy and practice* (pp. 261–283). Rotterdam, the Netherlands: Sense Publishers.

Statistics Canada. (2003). *Longitudinal survey of immigrants to Canada*. Retrieved from http://www23.statcan.gc.ca/imdb/p2SV.pl?Function=getSurvey&SDDS=4422&lang=en&db=imdb&adm=8&dis=2

Toronto Immigrant Employment Data Initiative (TIEDI). (2012). *TIEDI labour force update*. Retrieved from http://www.yorku.ca/tiedi/doc/lfs201208.pdf

Walsh, S., Brigham, S., & Wang, Y. (2011). Internationally educated female teachers in the neoliberal context: Their labour market and teacher certification experiences in Canada. *Teaching and Teacher Education*, 27, 657–665.

Xu, L. (2012). *Who drives a taxi in Canada?* Ottawa, ON: Citizenship and Immigration Canada. Retrieved from http://www.cic.gc.ca/english/pdf/research-stats/taxi.pdf

BONNIE L. SLADE *is a lecturer in adult education at the University of Glasgow, Scotland.*

The authors examine the U.S. contemporary immigrant and transnational migration phenomena and the historical immigrant experience using a postcolonial theoretical framework. In this chapter, the issues of race and gender and current political positions are discussed.

Race and Gender in Immigration: A Continuing Saga With Different Encryptions

Edward Joaquin, Juanita Johnson-Bailey

The United States, a country commonly recognized as a bastion of democracy and as a nation built and shaped by immigrants, ironically has a long and troubled history with immigration. In actuality that famous invitation written on the pedestal of the Statue of Liberty, "Give me your tired, your poor, your huddled masses yearning to breathe free" (Eiselein, 2002), was at best a conditional summons. Quite simply, it is because the United States is a nation of immigrants and therefore its citizenry lacks complete homogeneity as regards culture, religion, race, and ethnicity that our contemporary American existence is complicated. The early immigrants who melted into the great American pot became White, devoid of undesirable identifiers, such as skin color, language (other than English), customs, and other visible markers, and therefore were designated the settlers, the founding and developing members of this new colonial world (Novak, 1972); the present-day immigrants who similarly assimilate become the new contributors. In this chapter, we use a postcolonial perspective to assess and critique how the historically acquired colonial mindset shapes American society. Our standpoint is based theoretically apart from the insider's orthodox experience. Furthermore, we are outsiders, a voluntary and involuntary immigrant, a Filipino and an African American, who avail ourselves of our awareness as academics who exist on the margins, simultaneously enfranchised and disenfranchised, concurrently colonized and yet carrying a consciousness that recognizes societal power disparities.

We set forth that the American immigration chronicle is ongoing, as migration to the United States is not an issue of the past. Whereas the great migrations from Western and Northern Europe and from China and Japan are well known and researched historical events, the current migrations cannot be characterized as mass movements from specific geographical regions, but as a steady trickle from across the world that is admittedly having an impact on

New Directions for Adult and Continuing Education, no. 146, Summer 2015 © 2015 Wiley Periodicals, Inc.
Published online in Wiley Online Library (wileyonlinelibrary.com) • DOI: 10.1002/ace.20133

the United States in terms of resources and culture (Beneria, Deere, & Kabeer, 2012; Berg, 2013). It is estimated that 12% of the U.S. population was not born in the United States (Berg, 2013) and globally approximately 210 million people are classified as immigrants (International Labour Organization, 2010).

The Framework of U.S. Immigration Experiences

Historically, there have been amazing U.S. immigration stories and there have been terrible immigration stories, as not all immigrants have been equally welcomed and embraced by the United States citizens. The positive experiences of the English, French, and German immigrants are not the same as the experiences of the Irish residents or of the Eastern European people who came to the United States (Amott & Matthaei, 1999; Takaki, 2008). Similarly, the story of the Asian immigrant who came through Angel Island is not the Ellis Island tale of coming to America with no possessions but only a dream of a guaranteed second chance (Amott & Matthaei, 1999). For example the Chinese Exclusion Laws (1882–1943) prohibited all Chinese from entering the United States, except for merchants and their family, students, and diplomats (Amott & Matthaei, 1999; Arudou, 2013; U.S. Department of State Office of the Historian, 2014a).

Embedded within American immigration narratives are stories of voluntary and involuntary migration, states' anti-immigration restrictions, and federal laws that imposed quotas on Asian countries. For example, in the 1850s the state of California had Chinese Exclusion Laws, requiring special work permits and prohibiting naturalization for Chinese immigrants (U.S. Department of State Office of the Historian, 2014a). In the past the U.S. federal government has passed a succession of troubling laws, such as the Immigration and Nationality Act of 1952 (The McCarran–Walter Act), which has a section on Aliens and Nationality and upheld restrictive practices based on immigrant selection, giving preference to immigrants who were educated and skilled (U.S. Department of State Office of the Historian, 2014b).

The immigrants who came to the United States in the 1800s and 1900s were fulfilling the classic patterns if immigration as a one-way trip, with the immigrant population at the mercy of the host country, with few or no rights. The term transnationalism, which is routinely applied to the new immigrant, is an umbrella term used to reference a myriad of associations between immigrants and their home countries (Lee, 2011). This perspective of the one-way flow regarding immigration, migration, and/or transnationalism emerges from a colonial mindset, in which immigrants voluntarily abandon their home country and culture for a better life and spread across the world, establishing a diaspora, where people who share a culture and/or racial and ethnic bonds are connected through such ties despite geography. Yet using a postcolonial perspective, Mishra (2012) posits that, "Diasporics migrate to a new world not only physically and geographically, but also with their cultural artifacts and native consciousness" (p. 68). Therefore, immigration is both a set of figures and statistics and a theoretical frame (Morawska, 2003).

As an antecedent to understanding postcolonialism as a theoretical framework, the notion of colonialism must be taken into consideration as a point of reference. Memmi (1967) describes colonialism as one variety of totalitarianism: a movement, ideology, or attitude that favors dictatorial government, centralized control of private enterprise, and repression of all opposition; that is based on economics; and that justifies colonization to convert the indigenous people to becoming more civilized and pious to align with the same ideals of the colonizer.

A Colonial and Postcolonial Perspective on Immigration

Historically, colonialism included the acquisition of economics through the expansion of territories, the usurpation of natural resources, and the conquest of indigenous peoples as human capital. Such multifarious structures of industrialization resulted in a Western hegemony of political, social, and cultural ideologies that ultimately sustained power dynamics between the colonizer and the colonized (Prasad, 2003). Colonialism is a rudimentary form of a binary relationship contextualized to promote imperialism and sustain inequalities.

Loomba (2005) suggests postcolonialism as a period after colonialism, signifying the end of a colonial era. The term postcolonialism should be approached with an understanding of the perspective, context, and how *post* is derived and used in various writings. The use of *post* can be problematic to infer assumptions without properly deconstructing the laden power of its meaning. Without this understanding, its use may obfuscate un/intended meanings. It is hoped that this chapter will facilitate a productive interrogation of how we perceive our own contexts and positionalities in light of this topic.

The use of postcolonialism is an assumption from a privileged perspective that inaccurately attempts to eradicate colonial legacies by rhetorically atoning for and healing the relationship with the historically subjugated. The use of the term *post* also suggests an interrogation to whom and what purposes are being advanced and reproduced as reparations continually essentialize the characteristics central to colonialism and the colonial narrative. According to Ashcroft, Griffiths, and Tiffin (1995), "post-colonialism has an embedded discussion of varied experiences: migration, slavery, suppression, resistance, representation, difference, race, gender, and place. Additionally, post-colonialism has entrenched responses to the influential master discourses of imperial Europe such as history, philosophy, and linguistics, and the fundamental experiences of speaking and writing by which all these come into being" (p. 2). The distinction between the colonial and postcolonial worlds is not demarcated nor defined by a specific historical time period as many believe. The latent effects of colonization do not simply dissipate but are further perpetuated by the superiority/inferiority dichotomy or binary relationships that are endemic in many previously colonized cultures.

A postcolonial perspective facilitates the interrogation and deconstruction of these binary relationships to become conscious of how binary relationships are constructed and operate within domains of slavery, suppression, resistance, representation, difference, race, gender, and place. Given this, our working definition of postcolonial elicits the question of whether postcolonialism is a myth or a reality that has not yet been reconciled. Lastly, we should consider to whose *post* are we referring?

To help us do just this, we look at Foucault's idea of governmentality. Foucault offers a genealogy of governmentality that analyzes relationships between power and truth that propagate from shifts or discontinuities from historical events, which is analogous to colonialism to postcolonialism. Foucault's ideas are an intellectual challenge to meet a complex world situated in interrelated historical, economic, social, and political contexts, which are relevant to transnational immigrants. Foucault (2004) introduces governmentality as a complex idea, which he gradually explains:

> First, by "governmentality" I understand the ensemble formed by the institutions, procedures, analyses and reflections, the calculations and tactics that allow the exercise of this very specific complex form of power, which has as its target population, as its principal form of knowledge, political economy, and as its essential technical means apparatuses of security. (p. 108)

Foucault refers to an "ensemble" formed by the institutions that is not an orchestra or a band of musical performers but rather a collection of state and local agencies under the auspices of a superior institution. Foucault does not specifically define institutions in this context. However, we define institution as establishments that mandate certain rules and regulations. In other words, institutions have inherent power or control over the collaborative, analogous to an instructor (school) over a student or the Western beliefs over transnational migrants—in essence a reformation of a binary relationship. Foucault states that numerous procedures and calculations govern, uphold, and when necessary deploy tactics to ensure stability. By abiding by the rules and regulations, the target populations (transnational migrants) are guaranteed freedom and societal harmony. This method allows the government to function symbiotically throughout society.

Additionally, the term apparatus refers to a system that allows the government to function across multiple institutions such as schools and hospitals and these apparatuses use the devices of military techniques, police procedures, and various other governmental tactical powers (Holmes & Gastaldo, 2002). Western governments eventually replaced and shaped other forms of governance of colonized nations, such as sovereignty and discipline, into what society is today (Burchell, Gordon, & Miller, 1991). By governmentality, we understand the tendency, the line of force, which for a long time, and throughout the West, has constantly led toward the preeminence over all other types of power and knowledges of the colonized (Foucault, 2004, p. 108).

New Directions for Adult and Continuing Education • DOI: 10.1002/ace

The use of postcolonial theory as a lens to assess transnational migration and social inclusion first requires an understanding or at least some knowledge of the colonization from a historical aspect and identification of the transition from colonialism to a postcolonial era. Once this is determined, we can apply the postcolonial lens to better understand if postcolonialism is in effect or if colonialism is still relevant based on the experiences of individuals who transnationally migrate domestically and globally. This has a direct correlation to globalization and governmentality as it pertains to covertly disguised new forms of colonialism or neocolonialism. Because of the notion that colonialism is an idea of the past and that colonialism is not ongoing, the dialogue that ensues from postcolonialism puts us into a mindset that post is after the fact or that it no longer occurs. In other words, because there are no longer any colonized nations, the term colonial no longer applies, and thus we are led to believe and think in terms of a postcolonial society.

If there are no colonized nations or disenfranchised people, then all things are equal and nationality does not matter. If all differences are obscured, then other positionalities, such as race and gender, are no longer of significant concern. Instead, we will proceed to use a postcolonial framework as a lens through which to view immigration and transnational migration, with the standpoint of globalization representing the new face of colonialism. Postcolonialism allows us to critique the ongoing problematics of persistent colonialization. Although we separately discuss the significance of race and gender to past immigration and continuing transnational migration, we acknowledge the interconnectedness of these two systems of oppression.

Race and Immigration

The issue of immigration has generally been cloaked in the language of patriotism and nationalism and was stirred by peak periods when there was an arrival of large groups of people who were ethnically similar or from the same geographical area, the Irish in the 1850s or the Chinese in the 1870s. In the early years of the United States' centennial, immigrants arrived in great numbers: in the mid-1800s approximately 3 million Irish settled in Northeastern U.S. cities and in the latter part of the 1800s 12 million Chinese migrated to the Western United States. The debates over naturalizing the new residents centered on how their presence could affect the country. It was thought that a large immigrant population placed a threat on material resources, including taking American jobs. Additionally, part of the discussion was the notion that the "invading" groups were intellectually inferior, possessed an insufficient work ethic, and were prone to criminal behaviors (Mukherjee, Molina, & Adams, 2013). Overall, there was a national suspicion that an unchecked open door policy would damage the fabric of the nation.

The issues of race and the bias of racism were overtly present in the immigration discussions of the 1800s and the 1900s. Racism, as defined by critical race theory, is a system of power relations that established hierarchical categories based on physical characteristics allegedly tied to biological similarities within the disenfranchised group and their supposed dissimilarities to other groups, particularly the dominant group (Crenshaw, Gotanda, Peller, & Thomas, 1995; Ladson-Billings & Tate, 1995; Outlaw, 1996). However, the contemporary immigration debate in the United States, which focuses mostly on people from countries in the South, uses coded language (Hartman, Newman, & Bell, 2014). The concerns raised are over the violations of the law committed by people who enter the United States illegally, do not leave, and supposedly do not pay taxes. In fact, this is simply a new form of racism, referred to with different terms: modern racism, aversive racism, subtle prejudice, racial ambivalence, and symbolic racism (Berg, 2013). Modern racism, according to Hartman et al. (2014), is a catchall post–Civil Rights label for the racists who understand and abide by political correctness and therefore avoid overt expressions and acts of bias. So the days of exploiting a desperate and unprotected workforce (Takaki, 2008) by openly paying them half salary or Mexican wages (Montejano, 1987) have given way to other practices.

Overall, prejudice has become coded and wrapped in a new, less offensive language and discussion. These kinder and hypothetically gentler forms of oppressive beliefs are not based on theories of biological inferiority but instead stress the different between them and us, with them, the other being endowed with undesirable traits that stand them apart. According to Dietrich (2011), the colorblind perspective is new and different in that it is "characterized by subtle covert expressions of racism, including insinuations that today's racial inequalities reflect cultural deficiencies rather than systemic discrimination" (p. 727).

Granted, this is a different slant, the present-day debate also raises the points of limited material resources and jobs, the threat to the Christian (meaning Protestant) belief systems, and the possibility of deviant and criminal behavior on the part of the immigrants. In other words, there is talk of citizenship and culture but silence around the issue of race. The specter of group threat (Berg, 2013) looms large in the midst of the immigration debate, advancing the idea that the home team, native-born U.S. citizens (Whites) are the dominant ethnoracial group who have proprietorship over the nation's resources, land, and opportunities (Berg, 2013). When another group arrives and wants the same goods and prospects, then the dominant ethnoracial group feels exposed to the possibility of losing ground. In reaction to these feelings of vulnerability, the dominant group attempts to adjust laws and policies (Berg, 2013) to ensure that their advantages and privileges are maintained and passed on to their offspring.

The underlying issue that makes immigration a struggle for the ages is an economic one that straddles the tension between the colonial and the postcolonial standpoint. As regards earlier immigration patterns, when the United States had a demand for labor and resources were abundant, then the borders were open; when the demand was low and resources were scarce, then the borders slammed shut (Amott & Matthaei, 1999). In contrast, contemporary immigration is significantly affected by globalization and the erosion of borders and governments and the hastening of global reach in the acquisition of knowledge, capital, services, and people (Boccagni, 2012). This new migration, transnational migration, began to increase during the last 2 decades of the 20th century and was driven by globalization (Beneria et al., 2012) and by the changes in many countries in the South that were shifting from agriculturally based societies to urban societies.

Gender and Immigration

The issue of gender and sexism has always been extant in immigration and migration discussions. However, in earlier debates around the peoples who migrated to the United States in the 1800s and 1900s, the issue of gender appears secondary. Indeed, openly and widely expressed concern over the migration of women seems to have centered only on Asian women (Amott & Matthaei, 1999). Chinese, Japanese, and Filipino single males were recruited by the United States and paid low wages as a method of stimulating the economy, during the late 1800s and through the 1930s. The fear of Asian immigrant men and women procreating and thereby increasing their numbers was a tangible fear. One of the methods used to thwart the increase of Asians in the American populace was the use of miscegenation laws, the segregation codes, which prevented and regulated socializing and marriage between people of different races. If Asian men could not mix with and reproduce with White women, then there would be no Asian offspring. Another method used to control the Asian population was to forbid the migration of Asian women. For example, the Chinese Exclusion Act prohibited single Chinese women from coming to the United States (Arudou, 2013, U.S. Department of State Office of the Historian, 2014a). Although the pattern of migration for Japanese women was different, mainly because the government of Japan participated in controlling the migration of Japanese to the United States, there was still a severe imbalance between the numbers of men who came to the United States versus the smaller number of women who migrated, a 1 to 4 ratio (Amott & Matthaei, 1999). The migration of Chicana and Latina women is a different matter because of the proximity of the U.S. border to Mexico and Latin America. Yet, the colonial mindset about the place and position for women of color is seen across all migrant group experiences: women of color are subjected to sexual exploitation and were thought to be primarily suited for service work (Amott & Matthaei, 1999; Burn, 2011; Gianettoni & Roux, 2010; Lim, Smith, & Dissanayake, 1999).

In complete contrast to past immigration debates, the present-day discussion on immigration does consider gender (Burn, 2011; Gianettoni & Roux, 2010; Lim et al., 1999; Pajnik & Bajt, 2010). The inclusion of women in the immigration discussion seems to be necessitated by the fact that at least 50% of global immigrants are women. Transnational immigrant women are relocating not only because they want access to an *allegedly better* labor market but also because of family ties to partners and children (Burn, 2011; Pajnik & Bajt, 2010). So presently immigration has a different dimension than past immigration passages, as there is a feminization of the contemporary migration phenomenon. However, two persistent and continued themes that occur in both past and modern immigration are that women migrators are sexualized and are afforded lower paying jobs: sweatshop laborers, child and elder care workers, household maids (Amott & Matthaei, 1999; Burn, 2011; Gianettoni & Roux, 2010). In an extension of the colonial perspective, women migrants are classified as *followers*. Indeed Pajnik and Bajt (2010) state that women are viewed as having primary responsibility for forming and maintaining the family unit, the assumption being that women occupy the roles of nurturing and procreation. Pajnick and Bajt further assert that because of this gendered or sexist perspective, women are cast as family dependents with no independent legal standing. The positioning of women as secondary migrants and as lower paid immigrants has consequences for their well-being and their potential to fulfill their economic and civic needs or dreams.

This feminized migration has, according to Beneria et al. (2012), sponsored consideration of several issues: (a) what does it mean to be a transnational family; (b) how does migration and living across cultures affect family gender roles; and (c) how does the loss of the benefit from women's labor (both paid and unpaid) and the forfeiture of women's intellectual resources (brain drain) affect and alter the host nation? The literature on women and transnational migration does not attend to these issues, as a colonial mindset has given minor attention to the dimension of gender.

Education and Transnational Immigration

Although transnational education is not a new phenomenon, it is being drastically affected by globalization. As such, transnational education is increasing in complexity and there is no absolute definition or a body of literature on transnational education (Adam, 2001; van der Wende, 2003). A major development of transnational immigration has been an urgent need to increase the skills and educational levels of transnational migrant workers if they are to find a place in the workforce of the host country (van der Wende, 2003). This push for access has occurred in concert with the immigration pattern from South to North, as the educational levels in the socioeconomically disadvantaged South lag behind the educational and skill levels in the North. The need is not only for industrialized countries, like the United States, Canada, Australia, and Western European nations, but also included in this demand are the transitioning countries in Southeast Asia and Latin America that are entering into world production (van der Wende, 2003; World Bank, 2000).

The demand for educating the adult migrant population is not being filled by traditional higher education institutions because these institutions are ill equipped to accommodate the diverse groups' requirements and the immigrant population is rarely equipped to pay for traditional educational services. Therefore, adult education programs need to adapt their curriculum to educate learners about transnational immigrant education concerns and these programs must also infuse strategies that address the needs of immigrant students. Including both of these tactics will promote social inclusion. Additionally, according to the *Transnational Education Project Report and Recommendations*, a comprehensive European generated research report that analyzed transnational education in 17 European countries and Australia (Adam, 2001), major issues such as educational delivery, accreditation of educational programs, and failure of educational cultural matters to translate across cultures, adding to the quandary of how to operationalize high-quality transnational education. The problems identified in this report can direct adult education policy in order to provide a comprehensive approach.

Although the use of technology in the form of distance education and virtual universities is being offered as a possible solution for providing transnational education to the emerging market (Adam, 2001), we posit that this seems a possible continuation of globalization and colonialism as the flow of information is from Western countries. Furthermore, we contend that higher education and basic adult education extend to embrace transnational education as a promising opportunity for building a new market. Indeed doing so seems a logical extension of adult education's tenet of democratization (Cunningham, 1988).

References

Adam, S. (2001, March). *Transnational education project report and recommendations*. Westminster, UK: Confederation of European Union Rectors' Conference.

Amott, T., & Matthaei, J. (1999). *Race, gender and work: A multi-cultural economic history of women in the United States*. Boston, MA: South End Press.

Arudou, D. (2013). "Embedded racism" in Japanese migration policies: Analyzing Japan's "revolving door" work visa regimes under critical race theory. *Journal of Asia Pacific Studies, 3*(1), 155–185.

Ashcroft, B., Griffiths, G., & Tiffin, H. (1995). *The post-colonial studies reader*. London, UK: Routledge.

Beneria, L., Deere, C., & Kabeer, N. (2012). Gender and international migration: Globalization, development and governance. *Feminist Economics, 18*(2), 1–33.

Berg, J. A. (2013). Opposition to pro-immigrant public policy: Symbolic racism and group threat. *Sociological Inquiry, 83*(1), 1–31.

Boccagni, P. (2012). Rethinking transnational studies: Transnational ties and the transnationalism of everyday life. *Journal of Social Theory, 15*(1), 117–132.

Burchell, G., Gordon, C., & Miller, P. (Eds.). (1991). *The Foucault effect: Studies in governmentality*. Chicago, IL: University of Chicago Press.

Burn, S. M. (2011). *Women across cultures: A global perspective*. New York, NY: McGraw-Hill.

Crenshaw, K., Gotanda, N., Peller, G., & Thomas, K. (Eds.). (1995). *Critical race theory: The key writings that formed the movement*. New York, NY: The New Press.

Cunningham, P. M. (1988). The adult educator and social responsibility. In R. G. Brockett (Ed.), *Ethical issues in adult education* (pp. 133–145). New York, NY: Teachers College Press.

Dietrich, D. R. (2011). The specter of racism in the 2005–6 immigration debate: Preserving racial group position. *Critical Sociology*, 38(5), 723–745.

Eiselein, G. (2002). *Emma Lazarus: Selected poems and other writings*. Ontario, Canada: Broadview Press.

Foucault, M. (2004). *Security, territory, population: Lectures at the College de France, 1977–78* (M. Senellart, Ed., & G. Burchell, Trans.). New York, NY: Palgrave Macmillan. (Original work published 1978)

Gianettoni, L., & Roux, P. (2010). Interconnecting race and gender relations: Racism, sexism and the attribution of sexism to the racialized other. *Sex Roles*, 62, 374–386.

Hartman, T. K., Newman, B. J., & Bell, C. S. (2014). Decoding prejudice toward Hispanics: Group cues and public reactions to threatening immigrant behavior. *Political Behavior*, 36, 143–163.

Holmes, D., & Gastaldo, D. (2002). Nursing as means of governmentality. *Journal of Advanced Nursing*, 38(6), 557–565. doi:10.1046/j.1365-2648.2002.02222.x

International Labour Organization. (2010). *International labour migration. A rights-based approach*. Geneva, Switzerland: Author.

Ladson-Billings, G., & Tate, W. (1995). Toward a critical race theory of education. *Teachers College Record*, 97, 47–68.

Lee, H. (2011). Rethinking transnationalism through the second generation. *The Australian Journal of Anthropology*, 22, 295–313.

Lim, S. G., Smith, L. E., & Dissanayake, W. (1999). *Transnational Asia Pacific: Gender, culture, and the public sphere*. Chicago: University of Illinois Press.

Loomba, A. (2005). *Postcolonial studies and beyond*. Durham, NC: Duke University Press.

Memmi, A. (1967). *The colonizer and the colonized* (H. Greenfeld, Trans.). Boston, MA: Beacon Press. (Original work published 1965)

Mishra, R. K. (2012). Colonialism, post-colonialism, and diaspora in terms of translation. *The IUP Journal of English Studies*, 7(2), 61–69.

Montejano, D. (1987). *Anglos and Mexicans in the making of Texas, 1836–1986*. Austin, TX: University of Texas Press.

Morawska, E. (2003). Disciplinary agendas and analytic strategies of research on immigrant transnationalism: Challenges of interdisciplinary knowledge. *International Migration Review*, 37(3), 611–640.

Mukherjee, S., Molina, L. E., Adams, G. (2013). "Reasonable suspicion" about tough immigration legislation: Enforcing laws or ethnocentric exclusion? *Cultural Diversity and Ethnic Minority Psychology*, 19(3), 320–331.

Novak, M. (1972). *Rise of unmeltable ethnics*. New York, NY: Macmillan Publishers.

Outlaw, L. T. (1996). *On race and philosophy*. New York, NY: Routledge.

Pajnik, M., & Bajt, V. (2010). Migrant women's transnationalism: Family pattern and policies. *International Migration*, 50(5), 153–168.

Prasad, A. (2003). *Postcolonial theory and organizational analysis: A critical engagement*. New York, NY: Palgrave Macmillan.

Takaki, R. A. (2008). *A different mirror: A multicultural history of multicultural America* (2nd ed.). Boston, MA: Little, Brown, and Company.

U.S. Department of State Office of the Historian. (2014a). *Chinese immigration and the Chinese Exclusion Acts*. Retrieved from https://history.state.gov/milestones/1866-1898/chinese-immigration

U.S. Department of State Office of the Historian. (2014b). *The Immigration and Nationality Act of 1952 (The McCarran-Walter Act)*. Retrieved from https://history.state.gov/milestones/1945-1952/immigration-act

van der Wende, M. C. (2003). Globalisation and access to higher education. *Journal of Studies in International Education*, 7(2), 193–206.

World Bank. (2000). *Higher education in developing countries: Peril and promise*. Washington, DC: Author.

EDWARD JOAQUIN, a PhD graduate in adult education from the University of Georgia, USA, is a scholar who researches the postcolonial immigrant experience.

JUANITA JOHNSON-BAILEY is a professor of adult education and women's studies at the University of Georgia, USA.

This article explores how notions of diaspora, migration, and globalization intersect to inform identities and social realities of those who leave their homeland and resettle in other nations. It calls for expanding the discourse of adult education to incorporate critical studies of the diaspora to make visible the inequality and imbalance of power inherent in the process of migration and resettlement.

Diaspora, Migration, and Globalization: Expanding the Discourse of Adult Education

Mary V. Alfred

A review of the adult education literature reveals the glaring neglect of issues that affect the rapidly increasing number of foreign-born adults who take up residence in other countries, either through voluntary or through forced migration. Noting that adult and higher education programs are often a newcomer's first stop in accessing learning opportunities to aid in their transition and acculturation, these institutions are often out of touch with the realities of the global world as evidenced by their absence in the discourses on such issues (Alfred & Guo, 2012; Nesbit, 2005; Suarez-Orozco, 2007). According to Alfred and Guo (2012), because of the permeable nature of national borders, the speed of information flow, and the growing diversity of cultures, the movement of people and their connection to their home and host societies have wide implications for teaching and learning. Suarez-Orozco (2007), for example, asserted migration is the human side of globalization, and if that is ignored, we are ignoring the impact of globalization on individuals, groups, and communities of the diaspora. A major impact of globalization, according to Robertson and White (2007), is its contribution to inequality and imbalance of power among citizens of nation–states.

To continue to make these issues of contemporary migration visible, there is an emerging field of inquiry referred to as Diaspora Studies, with research engagement primarily among European and Australian scholars. As Tololyan (2007) noted, the study of diaspora is emerging as a multidisciplinary discourse, highlighting waves of migration, dispersion of ethnic minorities, and resettlement in geographical spaces away from the country of origin. Cohen (1997) advances a typology of diasporas, namely victims, trade, imperial, and cultural diasporas, each with varying realities of the resettlement experience

New Directions for Adult and Continuing Education, no. 146, Summer 2015 © 2015 Wiley Periodicals, Inc.
Published online in Wiley Online Library (wileyonlinelibrary.com) • DOI: 10.1002/ace.20134

and notions of identities and place. Such diversity of transitions and transformations has implications for teaching and learning in global societies. With social justice and equity as the hallmarks of adult education philosophy and practice, it is fitting that we engage in discourses that would make visible the realities of learners and educators from diaspora communities. The purpose of this article is to explore how notions of diaspora, migration, and globalization intersect to inform identities and lives of those who leave their homeland and resettle in other nations.

Defining Diaspora

Historically, the term diaspora was used to represent the forced exile of the Jewish people from their homeland and conjures such concepts as "migration or exile, nostalgia, perpetuation of original traditions, customs and languages, and a dream of return to the homeland" (Dufoix, 2011, p. 2). The central tenet of this view is the notion of forced migration from one's country of origin, maintenance of a national identity in the new homeland, and a dream of return to the home of origin. Viewing diaspora from this perspective, Safran (1991) maintains one can claim diaspora when several of these features can be applied:

- Individuals or their ancestors have been dispersed from one or more central geographic regions;
- They hold on to a collective memory (real or imagined), vision or myth about the original homeland;
- They believe that they are not and can never be fully accepted in their host societies and, therefore, partly separate themselves;
- They idealize their original home and believe that when conditions improve they or their descendants will return;
- They believe that all members of a diaspora should be committed to the maintenance of the ancestral home and contribute to its safety and prosperity; and
- They use various means to relate to the homeland and it is through this relationship that they remained consciously tied to home. (pp. 83–84)

Social scientists have taken issue with several of the precepts in Safran's definition of diaspora, particularly with the focus on territorial home for identification. For example, Brah (1996) discounts the concept of home as a fixed origin and, instead, embraces one's desire to remain connected to communities from the original homeland. I also contend that building and conceptualizing home within the territory of resettlement is an important consideration for defining diaspora. Another criticism of the traditional view is the lack of attention paid to ethnic and cultural diversity among diaspora communities when place of origin becomes the defining element. Similarly, Anthias (1998) questioned the fixed notion of origin and true belonging, instead advocating for diaspora discourse to make visible the internal divisions or the cultural negotiations that take place within ethnic communities of a diaspora. Diaspora communities are not homogeneous but diverse in many dimensions including race, ethnicity, gender, religious affiliation, and class, among others, and traditional diaspora ignores these forms of identification. This discontent with the traditional view paved the way for contemporary forms of theorizing the phenomena of border crossing, resettlement, and the definition of diaspora.

Conceptualizing Contemporary Diaspora

According to Dufoix (2011), contemporary diaspora has its roots in the evolutionary studies of the Black African Diaspora which started with British Cultural studies in the United Kingdom in the mid-1970s. This perspective shifted focus from the fixed and static space of homeland to the concepts of identity, communities, and cultural connection (Gilroy, 1997; Hall, 1990). Drawing from the Caribbean experience, Hall (1990) resists the notion of diaspora originating from fixed and static regions of Africa, thus giving Caribbean people an African homeland or a territorialized sense of belonging to Africa. Instead, he argues for the importance of conceptualizing the Caribbean experience as a "cultural production of Africa in the Caribbean, even if this production results in the search for African origins in Caribbean culture" (Dufoix, 2011, p. 3). To Hall, the word diaspora represents a heterogeneous group of immigrant people bind by common cultures of belonging and not necessarily by a fixed territorial place of beginning. From this perspective, central to the diaspora experience are elements of heterogeneity, diversity, and shifting identities. Diaspora identities, Hall claims, are those that are constantly producing and reproducing themselves through transformation and difference. Cohen (2007) supports Hall's assertion of heterogeneity and diversity in the concept, again using the Caribbean as an example; he explained, "Virtually all of those who settled in the Caribbean came from somewhere else—the African slave from West Africa, the White European settlers, planters and administrators from Europe, Indians arriving as the indentured workers from India and the traders from the Middle East" (p. 10). This diversity of points of origin and resettlement within ethnic groups make the traditional definition exclusive of most contemporary immigrants.

Although *home* remains central to the concept of diaspora, contemporary scholars are advocating that we expand the view of home to encompass new forms of mobility and displacement and the construction of new subjectivities and identities (Anthias, 1998; Brah, 1996; Cohen, 2007; Gilroy, 1997; Hall, 1990). To Brah (1996), home can be a placeless space that can be real or imagined. Similarly, Cohen (2007) concludes that the concept of "home" can be interpreted as a place of origin, the place of settlement, a national or transnational place, or an imagined virtual community linked by communication technologies or a matrix of known experiences and intimate social relations. An important argument against traditional diaspora is its macro approach with the nation as central as in the case of transnational discourse in the study of migration and resettlement. Transnational migration is often analyzed from a national framework but its strongest effects are felt at the local level—in communities, families, the job market, education and religious institutions, and political and social organizations, to name a few. Taking a transnational view distorts and renders invisible the ways by which diverse individuals and groups navigate challenging cultures, places, spaces, and practices at the micro level of homeplace. Arguing against the transnational approach, Anthias (1998) wrote,

> The lack of attention given to transethnic solidarities, such as those against racism, of class, of gender, of social movements is deeply worrying from the perspective of the development of multiculturality, and more inclusive notions of belonging. For a discourse of antiracism and social mobilization of a transethnic (as opposed to transnational) character, cannot be easily accommodated within the discourse of the diaspora, where it retains its dependence on "homeland" and "origin" however configured. (p. 577)

Central to the concept of diaspora is the movement and resettlement of people across nation–states; therefore, to capture the diversity of contemporary diaspora identities and communities, it is important to understand the forces of migration and how they intersect with globalization to shape this modern-day phenomenon.

Immigration and Modern Diaspora

As Guo (2013) noted, "Migration is a topic of great and enduring interest because almost every country is involved in this process as a source, transit or destination country, or indeed all three simultaneously" (p. 1). Similarly, Portes and Rumbaut (2006) see immigration as "a transformative force, producing profound and unanticipated social changes in both sending and receiving societies, in intergroup relations within receiving societies and among the immigrant themselves and their descendants" (p. xv). The reasons for leaving the homeland are diverse and result in different experiences with transition and resettlement. Whereas some groups come voluntarily in search of better economic and educational opportunities, others are pushed from their homelands because of war or political and civil unrests. Because of the different motivations for migration, Cohen (1997) argues that instead of viewing diaspora primarily as arising from a traumatic dispersal, we need to include those who come voluntarily transition from the homeland "in search of work, in pursuit of trade, or to further colonial ambitions" (p. 57). These circumstances give rise to various forms of diaspora, to include a labor diaspora, a trade diaspora, and an imperial diaspora (Cohen, 1997).

New Directions for Adult and Continuing Education • DOI: 10.1002/ace

Similarly, Portes and Rumbaut (2006) classified today's newcomers as labor migrants, professional immigrants, entrepreneurial immigrants, and refugees and asylees.

Regardless of the classification or condition of migration, scholars argue the motivation to voluntarily leave one's homeland has to do with the "push and pull" factor that fuels a life-altering decision to abandon a world that is known to take up residence in an unknown territory (Alfred, 2011; Guo, 2013; Portes & Rumbaut, 1996, 2006). Commenting on the phenomenon of U.S. migration, Portes and Rumbaut (1996) note:

> The basic reason why immigrants come to America is the gap between the life aspirations and expectations and the means to fulfill them in the sending countries. Different groups fill this gap with varying intensity, but it clearly becomes a strong motive for action. (p. 12)

Alfred (2011) has argued that the concept of the push and pull factors must be understood within the context of the material consumption of the West, which indeed motivates people to seek ways to partake in the materialism of industrialized nations. Easy access to communications technology has helped to accentuate the gap between life's conditions at home and those of more prosperous countries. Moreover, the ease of modern transportation has facilitated greater access to nations where these resources are more readily available. Portes and Rumbaut (2006) caution against drawing the conclusion that individuals at the lower end of the social strata from developing nations would be the ones most likely to be pulled by the materialism of developing nations. Instead, drawing from evidence from the United States, they note:

> Migration, in general, and the flow coming to the United States, in particular, do not originate mostly from the poorest of countries or most destitute regions. They often come from middle-income nations and among groups that are relatively advantaged with respect to the source population. This explains how the educational and skills credentials of the immigrant population of the United States at present are not much inferior to those of the native born. (p. 15)

Notably, when the data about immigrants and diaspora groups are disaggregated, the results indicate vast disparities in the skills and educational levels within and across members of sending nations. Some groups on average, for example, Asians, are more advanced educationally than those, for example, from the bordering nation of Mexico, highlighting the danger of conceptualizing diaspora and the various typologies as fixed phenomena. Another defining factor of today's immigrant population is the racial and ethnic composition of the newcomers. Unlike prior waves of migration that were primarily drawn from Europe, the majority of today's immigrants originate from non-Western nations, primarily from Asia, Latin America, Africa, and the Caribbean, thus leading to greater ethnic and cultural diversity among the U.S. population as is the case of other western nations. This increase in the ethnic minority population has implications for social inclusion and exclusion in a society, influenced by group membership. According to Castles (2000),

> Virtually every western country now has new ethnic minorities, which have risen through the migrations of the last fifty years. In some cases, descendants of immigrants may remain non-citizens even if born in the country of residence. Even those who are citizens may experience discrimination on the basis of race, ethnicity, or religion. Newly industrialized countries which import labor are trying to prevent the emergence of new minorities. Yet settlement often takes place anyway, leading to situations of marginalization, impoverishment, and social conflict. (p. 181)

Herein lies the contradiction of building national wealth and impoverishment simultaneously. As a result of globalization and deregulation of markets, the need for cheap labor from other nations to sustain a competitive economic advantage increased, while efforts to restrict their citizenship and resettlement through anti-immigration laws also took center stage. Therefore, individuals or groups who possess the necessary characteristics to fit into global markets are included into the new world order, with civil, political, and social rights, whereas those who do not fit are excluded and may be denied the most basic rights, such as the right to work and the right to food and security. Studies of diaspora and migration must burrow to the micro level to make visible the characteristics and identities of those included and excluded.

The Interdependence of Globalization and Migration

As previously noted, the competitive nature of the world economy propels the movement of people across national boundaries and requires multinational corporations and other migration regimes to facilitate such movement. In many countries, migration has been adopted as a strategy to compete for the most talented, skillful, and resourceful and to address their aging workforce (Guo, 2013). Moreover, globalization has been influenced by explosion of the communication and information revolution, together with the mobility of people, services, and goods. From a human dimension, migration continues to fuel the globalization phenomenon (Jones, 2000). To that end, migration and globalization are seen as interdependent phenomena. Similarly Guo (2013) noted, "Globalization and migration are inextricably intertwined. Where migration is a response to globalization, globalization accelerates migration" (p. 7).

Although nations welcome the phenomenon of globalization and the human and economic capital they enjoy, they resist the accompanying unwanted migration and resettlement that result from globalization. Some view this phenomenon with skepticism, whereas others see it as an inescapable world-wide occurrence with significant implications for the way we live our lives (Alfred, 2011). Regardless of one's position on globalization, it is a phenomenon that has resulted in drastic changes the world over, particularly in the areas of economics and culture, each with different consequences for different groups. As Stromquist and Monkman (2000) observed, the meaning of the term is fluid and varies depending on the area of emphasis within which it is being discussed. They noted:

> [Globalization] can be expressed in neoliberal economic perspectives, critical theory, and postmodernity. It has been applied to cover debates centering on convergence/divergence, homogenization/heterogenization, and local/global issues. Despite its ability to capture in its unfolding changes the involvement of the entire world in one way or another, globalization remains an inexact term for the strong, and perhaps irreversible, changes in the economy, labor force, technologies, communication cultural patterns, and political alliances it is imposing on every nation. (p. 3)

Indeed, much of the discourse focuses primarily on the dominant perspective of neoliberal globalization that is shaped by economic and geopolitical interests of rich powerful corporations and nations. Another view that is less advanced is that of cooperative globalization—the accumulation of human potentials with human development as its primary goal (Walters, 2000). This view of globalization has a bottom-up approach to development that is shaped by the basic needs of individuals and society. As Walters explains, "The proponents of this perspective argue that it is imperative for the very survival of the planet to find development alternatives to the neoliberal, competitive, and environmentally destructive economic and sociopolitical policies and practices that are dominating the world" (p. 199). Therefore, to counter the neoliberal effects of globalization, we need to center debates about globalization within the discourse of human development which calls for interventions from the bottom up (Jones, 2000; Walters, 2000). Such interventions must be sensitive to issues of gender, social justice, environment, community, and local culture, and they need to lead to financially and ecologically sustainable institutions (Walters, 2000). Therefore, the goal of development for the bottom-up approach should be the development of human capacities. Noting we live and learn in neoliberal, capitalistic societies where the accumulation of financial capital resources are fundamental to such societies, the question that remains unanswered is how can education, especially adult and higher education, help adults develop capacities to challenge and counter the negative effects of neoliberal globalization, and at the same time develop the skills and competencies necessary to compete within such environments. Viewing globalization from the bottom up provides an opportunity for adult education to be part of the discourse and opens space for analyses of global citizenship and belonging in and out of the diaspora.

New Directions for Adult and Continuing Education • DOI: 10.1002/ace

Citizenship and Diaspora: A Critical Perspective on Identity and Belonging

In adult education, *social justice for all* are buzzwords that guide the theory and practice of the discipline. Yet, despite the increase of transnational migration and the impact of globalization, scant evidence exist to suggest people of the diaspora have received much attention in the discourse of U.S. adult higher education. Alfred and Guo (2012) reported the findings of a study that examined the level of scholarly engagement among Canadian and U.S. adult educators. The study, conducted in 2009, found scant evidence of scholarly engagement on international issues, highlighting the static nature of attention to immigration and globalization. Similar observation was noted in analysis of the curricular content of the field. As a result, Alfred and Guo called for the development of global citizenship for social justice in civil society. In advancing the agenda for the development of global citizenship, the authors failed to critically analyze how identity and place informed citizenship for members of diaspora communities. As Rosaldo (1999) noted, citizenship is often understood as a universal concept where all citizens of a nation have equal rights and access under the law. Drawing from the author's work on the cultural citizen project in California, Texas, and New York, she highlights the importance of distinguishing "the formal level of theoretical universality from the substantive level of exclusionary and marginalizing practices" (p. 253). In other words, she is contesting the taken-for-granted assumptions of everyday terminology and highlighting the need to be critical about how these terms are operationalized in privileging and marginalizing different groups of individuals within a particular society. Heeding this challenge, I use critical theory as a conceptual tool to interrogate the notion of *citizenship* for people of the diaspora. The assumption that undergirds critical theory is that inequity is a permanent structural reality that is readily accepted because dominant ideology has convinced the majority that inequity is normal and predictable (Brookfield, 2010).

Being critical about the concept of citizenship situates the intersecting phenomenon of immigration, globalization, and diaspora within the critical discourse germane to adult education. As Brookfield (2010) observed, "Adult education conceived as critically reflective practice is built on the traditions of democratic pragmatism and Freirean praxis to explore how adults came to recognize and subvert power dynamics and how they came to acknowledge and challenge hegemony" (p. 72). Learning how to challenge hegemonic practices around issues of identity and belonging is an explicit part of the adult education agenda.

The identity of citizen, up to the early 20th century, was relegated to men of privilege with the rest of society identified as second class or noncitizens. This tyranny of social distinction of belonging continues to trickle down to contemporary societies where identity and citizenship remain contested terrains of inclusion and exclusion. Although the universal notion of citizenship was meant to be a symbol of democracy, the exclusionary practices in

New Directions for Adult and Continuing Education • DOI: 10.1002/ace

contemporary society continue to deprive a large percentage of the population of that *citizenship* by denying them the same rights and access as the privileged majority. Cultural citizenship operates in an uneven field of structural inequalities where the dominant claims of universal citizenship assume powerful White male identities and are usually blind by the exclusions and marginalization of people whose identities differ from those of the majority. Using a critical approach to global citizenship interrogates this dominance and alienation while paying attention to and making visible the agency and aspirations of those at the margins, to include members of diaspora communities who are essentially ethnic communities. As Tololyan (2007) reminds us, "All diaspora communities are ethnic communities, but not all ethnic communities are diasporic; diasporics are a specific subset of ethnic minorities" (p. 648). Therefore, researching and teaching of the diaspora must be anchored in the realities and perceptions of people who occupy subordinate social spaces.

Taking a critical approach to the concept of citizenship challenges educators and critical theorists to pay attention to the point of view of the populations they research or educate. Oftentimes, social scientists and educators anchor their epistemologies and pedagogical frameworks within the experiences of the dominant social group, thus rendering the less privileged as the "Other" from whose experiences they develop models and frameworks that render them as a problem rather than people with agency. According to Rosaldo, inequality and social position are reminders that people in different and often unequal positions have different understandings and realities of a given context. This is not to claim that members of a particular diaspora have the same understanding of a given experience but to caution against homogenizing an experience to be that of all members of a particular community.

Conclusion: Agenda for Adult Education

Situating the study and teaching of diaspora within the discourse of adult education creates space for an agenda for the deconstruction of assumptions that equate globalization primarily with progress and economic empowerment and, instead, replace it with new ways of understanding structure, agency, and social change as they relate to human development and the quest for identity and place of belonging. This agenda for research and teaching would be grounded in what Hickling-Hudson (2000) terms postmodern radical development theory and what Jones (2000) and Walters (2000) refer to as globalization from the bottom up. As Hickling-Hudson (2000) explains, "This new practice would be based on ecological and people-centered thinking, the critical use of appropriate technologies, the recognition and fostering of local and traditional knowledge, the strengthening of social movements for community empowerment, and research grounded in practice" (p. 220). With this agenda, race and ethnicity along with class and gender continue to matter because the vast majority of immigrants are from non-European and non-English-speaking regions of the world. Moreover, because of the intersection of globalization and

New Directions for Adult and Continuing Education • DOI: 10.1002/ace

immigration in shaping modern-day diasporas, research and teaching of identity, citizenship, and the politics of belonging make visible the sociocultural contexts of learners' lives—knowledge that has been established as critical to creating inclusive environments for learning in adult higher education.

References

Alfred, M. V. (2011). Adult higher education at the intersection of globalization, internationalization, and social justice. *Explorations in Higher Education Series, 1*, 11–18.

Alfred, M. V., & Guo, S. (2012). Toward global citizenship: Internationalization of adult education of Canada and the US. *The Canadian Journal for the Study of Adult Education, 24*(2), 51–70.

Anthias, F. (1998). Evaluating diaspora: Beyond ethnicity. *Sociology, 32*(3), 557–571.

Brah, A. (1996). *Cartographies of diaspora: Contesting identities.* New York, NY: Routledge.

Brookfield, S. D. (2010). Theoretical frameworks of understanding the field. In C. E. Kasworm, A. D. Rose, & J. M. Ross-Gordon (Eds.), *Handbook of adult and continuing education* (pp. 71–81). Thousand Oaks, CA: Sage.

Castles, S. (2000). Globalization and migration: Some pressing contradictions. *International Social Science Journal, 50*(156), 179–186.

Cohen, R. (1997). *Global diasporas: An introduction.* Seattle: University of Washington Press.

Cohen, R. (2007). Solid, ductile and liquid: Changing notions of homeland and home in diaspora studies. *QEH Working Paper Series, 156*, 1–17.

Dufoix, S. (2011). From nationals abroad to diaspora: The rise and progress of extra-territorial and over state nations. *Diaspora Studies, 4*(1), 1–20.

Gilroy, P. (1997). Diaspora and the detours of identity. In K. Woodward (Ed.), *Identity and difference* (pp. 299–348). London, UK: Sage.

Guo, S. (Ed.). (2013). *Transnational migration and lifelong learning: Global issues and perspectives.* New York, NY: Routledge.

Hall, S. (1990). Cultural identity and diaspora. In J. Rutherford (Ed.), *Identity, community, culture & difference* (pp. 222–237). London, UK: Lawrence & Wishart.

Hickling-Hudson, A. (2000). Globalization and universities in the commonwealth Caribbean. In N. P. Stromquist & K. Monkman (Eds.), *Globalization and education* (pp. 219–236). Lanham, MD: Rowman & Littlefield Publishers.

Jones, P. W. (2000). Globalization and internationalism: Prospects for world education. In N. P. Stromquist & K. Monkman (Eds.), *Globalization and education* (pp. 27–42). Lanham, MD: Rowman & Littlefield Publishers.

Nesbit, T. (2005). No direction home: A book review essay. *Adult Education Quarterly, 56*(1), 71–78.

Portes, A., & Rumbaut, A. G. (1996). *Immigrant America: A portrait* (2nd ed.). Berkeley, CA: University of California Press.

Portes, A., & Rumbaut, A. G. (2006). *Immigrant America: A portrait* (3rd ed.). Berkeley, CA: University of California Press.

Robertson, R., & White, K. E. (2007). What is globalization? In G. Ritzer (Ed.), *The Blackwell companion to globalization* (pp. 54–66). Malden, MA: Blackwell Publishing.

Rosaldo, R. (1999). Cultural citizenship, inequality, and multiculturalism. In R. D. Torres, L. F. Miron, & J. X. India (Eds.), *Race, identity, and citizenship: A reader* (pp. 253–261). Malden, MA: Blackwell Publishing.

Safran, W. (1991). Diaspora in modern societies: Myths of homeland and return. *Diaspora, 1*(1), 83–95.

Stromquist, N. P., & Monkman, K. (2000). Defining globalization and assessing its implication on knowledge and education. In N. P. Stromquist & K. Monkman (Eds.), *Globalization and education* (pp. 3–26). Lanham, MD: Rowman & Littlefield Publishers.

Suarez-Orozco, M. M. (2007). Wanted: Global citizens. *Educational Leadership*, 64(7), 58–62.

Tololyan, K. (2007). The contemporary discourse of diaspora studies. *Comparative Studies of South Asia, Africa and the Middle East*, 27(3), 647–655.

Walters, S. (2000). Globalization, adult education, and development. In N. P. Stromquist & K. Monkman (Eds.), *Globalization and education* (pp. 197–218). Lanham, MD: Rowman & Littlefield Publishers.

MARY V. ALFRED *is a professor of adult education in the College of Education and Human Development at Texas A&M University, USA.*

9

This chapter summarizes the key themes across the articles on transnational migration, social inclusion, and adult education, using Nancy Fraser's framework of redistributive, recognitive, and representational justice.

Rethinking Social Justice and Adult Education for Welcoming, Inclusive Communities: Synthesis of Themes

Elizabeth Lange, Catherine Baillie Abidi

With the rise of anti-Semitism in Germany and Europe, Jewish refugees hurriedly left their belongings, homes, and communities to escape the continent. These refugees implored in vain to many countries to open their doors to immigrants, to avoid catastrophic consequences. In 1939, the refugee steamship SS St. Louis was barred from disembarking in Cuba and the United States. Despite appeals from some sectors of Canadian society that favoured their admittance into the country, Canada also refused. The ship was forced to return to Europe. Years later, some of the [937] passengers were unaccounted for, and [at least 300] are believed to have perished in the Holocaust.
(Government of Canada, 2006, para. 1; Ogilvie & Miller, 2006)

Migration has been a persistent part of human history, whether for securing access to food and water or trading routes, or as a result of human aggression. Although people have always been on the move, contemporary complexities of migration have been compounded by historically shifting political, social, and geographic borders. In the age of the nation–state, nations imply boundaries, and boundaries imply that some are considered citizens and some strangers, some belong and some are excluded (Kelley & Trebilcock, 2010). Further, dependent on the dominant national narrative in each historical moment, immigration practices have been exclusionary, based on race, religion, gender, sexual orientation, ability, country of origin, language, education, social class, and/or economic wealth. Similar to those aboard the SS St. Louis, countless immigrants and refugees have been denied opportunities for migration and citizenship, protection from persecution, and access to needed support services and opportunities in a new country.

New Directions for Adult and Continuing Education, no. 146, Summer 2015 © 2015 Wiley Periodicals, Inc.
Published online in Wiley Online Library (wileyonlinelibrary.com) • DOI: 10.1002/ace.20135

With neoliberalism and the expansion of capital globally, immigration is again reaching historic highs, in terms of overall numbers and particularly in forced migration. Furthermore, transportation and communication advances are shifting global migration patterns toward transnationalism, where migrants maintain ties to the country of origin and transit countries, as well as the receiving nation. These contemporary transitions in migration require the adult education community to engage in deep and critically reflective dialogue about the scale of social justice and social inclusion.

The purpose of this chapter is to provide a summary of key themes in this issue and to synthesize them within a theoretical frame. Historically, the geographical integrity and goals of each nation–state were to be respected through nonintervention in internal affairs. With globalization, however, the scale of justice now needs to be considered transnational, as transborder injustices include environmental issues and climate events, predatory capital and corporate dispossession, terrorism and international security, diseases such as Ebola and HIV/AIDS, technology issues such as genetic modification, population dislocations and further creation of diasporas, and superpowers acting unilaterally eclipsing international processes (Fraser, 2009). As well, there are many new transnational actors, such as global social movements, intergovernmental organizations, and nongovernmental organizations. These evolving realities require adult educators to rethink social justice generally, and specifically in relation to newcomers. We use Nancy Fraser's (2009) three dimensional framework of justice—redistributive, recognitive, and representational—to tease out themes in previous chapters.

As disclosure, our interest as the authors of this issue emerges from a familial experience of migration, either as first, second, or third generation immigrants, joining a newcomer family through marriage, or as descendants of those forcibly moved by the slave trade. It is this generational experience of inclusion and exclusion that informs our adult education theory and practice toward social and economic inclusion.

Three Historical Waves of Migration and National Self-Interest

Although humanitarian concerns may inform the immigration policies of nation–states, national self-interest has been and continues to be the key driver. Nation-centered priorities are evident in each of the three waves of migration over the past few centuries, as argued by Hanlon and Vicino (2014).

First Wave. The first wave was the era of colonial expansion from the 17th to 19th centuries that included the migration of free people (people of wealth, artisans, farmers, craftspeople, and former military) as well as slaves, convicts, and indentured servants. The European-based colonizers (notably Britain, Spain, Portugal, the Netherlands, Belgium, Russia, Turkey, and France) jostled each other for control over Africa, Asia, the Middle East, and the Americas. Under the system of preindustrial mercantilism, cheap or free labor was used in mines, plantations, and other raw resource industries for European

New Directions for Adult and Continuing Education • DOI: 10.1002/ace

commodity production. It is in this colonial context that Joaquin and Johnson-Bailey (Chapter 7) as well as Alfred (Chapter 8) discuss the creation of diasporas, where dislocated people share a culture, collective memory, and/or racial and ethnic bonds across geography. As Alfred details, the original notion of diaspora from the colonial era has now expanded to include a typology of diasporas—labor diasporas, trade diasporas, and cultural diasporas—created by the push and pull factors of migration. These diasporas are important to the engagement of identity in adult education, yet, as the Caribbean experience of mixed ethnic and cultural origins exemplifies, a fixed sense of a homeland and homogenous identity can be difficult. Dialogue about such cultural negotiations at the micro level of place is important not only for the visibility of inclusion/exclusion dynamics but for developing more inclusive concepts of belonging and home as well as multiple, flexible identities.

Second Wave. The second wave of migration, during the industrialization era, intensified in the mid-19th century, expanding the colonial reach and peaking in numbers in the 1920s. Within Europe, there was a substantial movement of rural people to urban, industrializing areas as part of land dispossession still occurring in the Global South today. Two world wars also dislocated populations who moved again during postwar rebuilding. In addition, faster and cheaper travel by steamship and rail enabled "unskilled" Europeans to move en masse to North and South America and Australasia, driven by famine, continuous war, and recruiters appealing to the desire for land and religious freedom. Immigrants flooded into factories, coal mines, and steel mills or onto land opened up for farming through the forced dislocation and attempted genocide of Indigenous nations. As Joaquin and Johnson-Bailey (Chapter 7) describe, the U.S. 1886 Statue of Liberty represented a promise to immigrants built on the Enlightenment political ideas of individual equal worth and basic liberty. Yet, the economic goals of national expansionism and industrial prosperity contradicted the political goals, privileging the value of private property and the protection of racial privilege.

As all authors in this collection recount, immigration policy in settler countries was very restrictive in the attempt to build a homogenous society based on Anglo-Western European values and traditions. Australia's de facto "White only" policy enacted in the Immigration Restriction Act of 1901 attempted to retain the character of Australia as a British outpost, a policy changed only in the 1970s (Hanlon & Vicino, 2014). The Canadian Chinese Act of 1923 and the U.S. Chinese Exclusion Laws (1882, 1892, 1902) highlight the explicit prohibition of Chinese migrants, with the exception of those with money. Finally, during the world wars, the incarceration or deportation of those of "enemy-alien" birth and the exclusion of, or quotas for, "undesirable" migrants in many nations illustrate how fragile the rights of immigrants have been (Kelley & Trebilcock, 2010).

In terms of settlement and adult education, Shan (Chapter 2) details that services were originally provided by companies (typically trading and railway), churches, ethnic organizations, and settlement houses. For example,

Jane Addams's settlement house in Chicago offered night school for the neighborhood immigrant population while advocating for social reform. Similarly, Alfred Fitzpatrick's Frontier College offered evening literacy classes to laborers, often immigrants, using university students as laborer–teachers, in far flung Canadian bush camps associated with mining, logging, or railway construction. As Shan elaborates, although social reform informed Fitzpatrick's intentions, so did Christian values and the goal of "civilizing" newcomers, part of a larger paternalistic framework. Other adult education examples are university extension, which intended to "civilize" rural populations through circuit-riding professors teaching literacy and education; the Mechanics Institutes, which offered scientific knowledge, technical skills, and values of industriousness and punctuality to the new laboring class; the YMCA, which offered moral discipline and character training for laborers caught in the dislocation to dirty, degrading, crowded cities and dehumanizing factory work; and the Danish Folk Schools, which offered cultural revivalism for democratization and economic stimulus. Thus, adult education has historically been complicit in the assimilationist paradigm.

Early Third Wave. Outrage at the travesties of the Nazi regime, restrictive immigration policies during the world wars, and the postwar need for family reunification influenced the third wave of migration after the Second World War. Formed in 1945, the United Nations is dedicated to international peacekeeping, cooperation, and human rights, and has crafted numerous conventions and treaties aimed at protecting global human, political, civil, social, cultural, and economic rights. Thus, the geopolitical and ideological context began to change, resulting in increased concern for international poverty and development. This ideological shift was momentous and can be considered a form of redistributive justice in which justice was understood as the removal of barriers to create "parity of participation" based on the principle of equal moral worth (Fraser, 2009). Justice in this sense is economic justice where social goods are more evenly distributed and opportunity structures more available so that all have a chance to contribute to society no matter what their circumstances have been.

From the mid-20th century, decolonization and newly independent nations changed the immigrant source countries and created a demographic shift from European migrants to Global South migrants. Civil rights and antiracist sentiments emerged, yielding a more humanitarian approach to immigration policies and a reevaluation of preferential, discriminatory, and racialized selection systems. Shan (Chapter 2) defines this as the shift from an assimilative to integration ideology, where integration is defined as an ongoing process of mutual accommodation between an individual and society. Through integration policies, the goal is for immigrants to have the ability to contribute to every aspect of their new country—economic, social, cultural, and political—free of barriers (Government of Canada, 2001, 2010). Countries such as Canada, Australia, and Aotearoa/New Zealand began to adopt official multicultural policies, recognizing themselves as countries of racial and ethnic diversity. At the same time, with growing demographic diversity in most Northern countries, and with new social movements and multiculturalism discourse, justice concerns shifted to recognition. Recognitive justice challenges hierarchies of cultural value that deny some and privilege others (Fraser, 2009).

Yet, Shibao Guo (Chapter 1) and Yan Guo (Chapter 4) emphasize that the ideological shift to recognitive social justice is not necessarily manifested in practice. Residential segregation, poor educational outcomes, un- or underemployment, political alienation, credential devaluation, downward social mobility, marginalization of immigrant women into a cheap, docile labor force, and exploitative volunteer programs are just some of the evidence that, as S. Guo puts it, "difference as deficit" still exists and newcomers are excluded from full membership and inclusion. Further, as various authors discuss, some types of knowledge, language, and power continue to be privileged and others marginalized. As Americans Joaquin and Johnson-Bailey (Chapter 7) assert, colonialism is an obscured but persistent mindset, and race is implicit within discussions of citizenship and culture.

Late Third Wave. Since the 1990s, however, the more liberal, humanitarian approach to immigration has been systematically eroded as economic priorities have surged to the fore. National self-interest now explicitly drives the immigration tap—turned on in times of prosperity and turned off in times of economic constraint and fear (Stalker, 2001). The utilitarian use of migration for economic sustainability is not new; however, the resurgence of migration within economic discourse and class privilege has resulted in a divergence from the humanitarian and family reunification foci of previous years. As Alfred (Chapter 8) explains, enhanced mobility and the unevenness of global economics provide motivation for people to seek out higher income, material wealth, and life opportunities in the Global North, sometimes as a family or community strategy (Stalker, 2001).

As Alfred (Chapter 8) and S. Guo (Chapter 1) argue, neoliberal globalization and migration are tightly linked, including competing for the most talented and educated immigrants. Even so, in Canada for example, immigrants who are better educated, in better health, and at similar career stages as Canadian-born people have been experiencing less successful integration over the last 20 years (Wayland, 2006). Further, not only economic globalization, but the September 11, 2001 attacks on the United States have generated increasingly exclusionary and securitized state policies, with important implications for the field of adult education.

Current Trends of Exclusion

The denial of the SS St. Louis may appear at odds with humanitarian and multicultural narratives, but exclusionary policies and practices are again rising, even in the context of growing transnational migration and a 25-year high in forced migration. Neoliberal globalization has produced policies for "designer immigrants" selected for their professional and potential economic productivity, as nations position themselves as "sophisticated, knowledge-worker-based global trader[s]" (Simmons, 2010, p. 83). As demonstrated by Slade (Chapter 6), the "professionalization of migration" is a strategic endeavor to accomplish national aspirations for economic excellence. Overwhelming immigration research confirms that family reunification is the key to success-ful integration where "extended families are the anchors and generators of chains of migration" and the links to social capital and professional networks (Dobrowolsky & Ramos, 2014, p. 31). Yet, the "prevailing econocentric ap-proach" to immigration policy does not account for these social and cul-tural realities and other dimensions of life beyond the economic (p. 27). Furthermore, the expansion of temporary foreign worker programs has created modern forms of labor exploitation and undermined labor standards and pro-tections. Migration policies now generate dual labor markets with two types of jobs—secure, high skilled, and well paid; and 3D jobs, which are dirty, dangerous, and difficult (Stalker, 2001), with women and young people over-represented in 3D jobs.

Since 9/11, nation–states have additional restrictive measures to pro-tect national security and harmonize border policies. Current discourse links migration and terrorism, generating deportation provisions that are often in violation of the Geneva Convention of 1951, and which criminalize or dele-gitimize asylum seekers requesting protection. Contemporary refugee poli-cies often accuse asylum seekers of being "queue-jumpers" who abuse welfare systems, intensifying their persecution. Increased racial profiling at borders, deterrence efforts at airports, and the ability to revoke citizenship at any time further illustrate the modern-day racism, sexism, and militarism im-plicit in migration policies. In the U.S. context, Joaquin and Johnson-Bailey (Chapter 7) demonstrate that the diverse "welcomes" afforded to migrant groups and the "coded language" embedded within migration policies aim to exclude and maintain racist practices, but, as Jakubowski (1997) says, they are communicated in ways that can be publicly defensible. Thus, not only can migration policies prohibit the migration of certain people from cer-tain places, the request for protection or the attainment of citizenship does not necessarily secure citizenship rights. These exclusionary trends—prior to citizenship, during citizenship determination, and now postcitizenship—are worrisome.

With the erosion of the welfare state, many settlement programs have become heavily reliant on cost-recovery or user pay systems, taken out of future individual earnings or covered through sponsorships, highlighted by Shan (Chapter 2). Brigham, Baillie Abidi, Tastsoglou, and Lange (Chapter 3) identify the reduction in the acceptance of refugees and the elimination or stark reduction of social assistance for those without refugee status, magni-fying the vulnerability of an already underserved population. As global in-equality reaches record gaps, redistributive justice and recognitive justice have been losing ground. As Fraser (2009) argues, this calls for a reframing of justice.

Adult Education for Newcomers: Realities, Restrictions, and Challenges

Adult education has been tightly linked with migration, particularly since the great migrations of the late 19th and early 20th centuries, and is now embedded within the phenomenon of transnational migration in multiple and complex ways. As migrants move within and beyond borders, they bring a wealth of learning experiences and cultural perspectives. Given the social justice underpinnings of adult education historically, current practices in migration settlement require critical reflection among practitioners as well as a shift toward asset-based practices, which recognizes and values the abilities, strengths, experiences, and knowledge systems of migrants.

Unfortunately, as Gibb (Chapter 5), Slade (Chapter 6), and others identify, programming that serves migrant communities still stems from a deficit model. Increased learning on the part of migrants (i.e., language acquisition and employment skills) occupies the central focus of government funding and thus the focus of settlement services. Guo (2010) argues that this denigrates prior learning and work experience. Shan (Chapter 2) highlights that while settlement programs are important sites for learning, strength-based approaches are faltering due to funding obligations that favor employment preparation programs. Slade and Gibb (Chapters 6 and 5) argue that these shifts result in either the repetitive training or "deprofessionalization" of migrants where they settle for jobs outside their specialized training and often at low-skilled levels, resulting in downward mobility.

Gibb (Chapter 5) refers to this process as the "managerial enterprise," or the move from community-centered settlement support and education, to employment preparation. According to Gibb, this deficit approach to migrants in relation to language has significant implications as language learning becomes more singularly connected to employability. Gibb also identifies that regimes of testing and benchmarking are now commonplace on the global scene, driven by agencies such as the Organisation for Economic Co-operation and Development (OECD) and transnational researchers, practitioners, and policymakers. Increasingly, migrant entry is contingent on these tests of competence, sifting people in the war for talent. Yet, language is not a fixed system but is highly contextual within localized social activities, and the relationship between written text and spoken language is complex. Thus, she argues, both literacy and language education are cultural, political, and ideological constructs that continue to exclude "other" knowledge cultures. Literacy and language education are now too often *not* about empowerment or civic participation but about employability and earnings.

Even so, Slade (Chapter 6) argues that skilled migration assumes ease of labor market integration, yet this is not often realized. Labor market exclusion is embedded in lack of credential recognition, restrictive licensing processes, devaluation of international work experience, professional barriers, and a racialized and gendered labor market that selects people of color and minority women for low income sectors. This results in the "occupational skidding" of immigrants who gain job experience outside their field of training but who, over time, lose touch with their professions and are never able to return. New programs of volunteering to gain work and language experience typically do not improve their labor position but are complicit in taking immigrants away from their field of training and level of education and, in some cases, exploiting their labor. In addition, the onus and responsibility for learning is placed on individual migrants, despite the reality that most migrants have limited access to sites of nonformal and formal learning (Guo, 2010). By placing the burden of settlement and transition solely on migrants, issues of power, inequitable social structures, and diverse social capital are pushed beneath the surface and not taken up within the development of migration policy and adult educational practices.

Adult education within the settlement sector is highly influenced by the neoliberal ideologies of funders and is increasingly becoming a surveillance culture to ensure economic priorities are privileged. Burstein and Esses (2012) argue that organizations offering settlement support to immigrants "generally lack the fiscal room to conduct detailed analyses of their actions . . . the result is that excellent local initiatives suffer from 'locked-in syndrome,' and the sector as a whole lacks an effective strategy for sharing information efficiently and learning from each other" (p. 4). Still, many nongovernmental organizations are known to offer literacy and language training to refugee claimants, even though policies and funding are meant to restrict access. So, service providers find themselves split between humanitarian responses and policy mandates, part of the emotional toll among service providers that Brigham, Baillie Abidi, Tastsoglou, and Lange (Chapter 3) discuss.

The failure to develop migration policy from a critical perspective results in funding and programmatic restrictions that continue to oppress certain groups of immigrants. In particular, Shan (Chapter 2), Slade (Chapter 6), and Joaquin and Johnson-Bailey (Chapter 7) highlight the gendered nature of migration policies and the ways in which gender is excluded from consideration in migration settlement practices. The lack of gendered analysis in settlement work is problematic given the differential impact by gender, argue Tastsoglou, Baillie Abidi, Brigham, and Lange (2014). Another underserved population in adult education is settlement service providers, who daily navigate shifting policies and practices. Constant informal learning is required within settlement services to do their jobs, particularly in the context of continuously shifting federal migration and refugee policies. The emphasis on assimilation versus integration is also evident in the lack of formal adult education for the settlement sector as well as for migrants with regard to migration policy and integration.

Guo (2010) argues that lifelong learning can serve as a "barrier and a gatekeeper, and by extension, a means of social control and subordination" (p. 162). Adult education within migration requires a critical lens to explore how "barriers" and "gatekeepers" form and influence the overall migration experiences of immigrants. It also calls for what Fraser identifies as representational justice. Representational justice incorporates a political dimension and "tells us who is included in, and who [is] excluded from, the circle of those entitled to a just distribution and reciprocal recognition" (Fraser, 2009, p. 17).

Rethinking Social Justice and Adult Education for Inclusive Communities

Despite the growing exclusionary trends in the midst of increased transnational migration and the complicity of adult education in assimilationist, econocentric, and managerialist approaches, the authors offer many recommendations for the field of adult education that can enhance redistributive, recognitive, and representational justice.

As argued by Shan (Chapter 2), "two-way integration" is essential for the development of welcoming and inclusive communities, where both immigrants and receiving communities are involved in mutual accommodations. Integration is fostered through civic engagement, social interaction particularly with dominant groups, labor market participation with income and educational parity, and community relationships that foster social efficacy and trust. Adult education has the unique opportunity of acting as cultural brokers, says Y. Guo (Chapter 4). Cultural brokering is the act of bridging, linking, and mediating between groups and persons of differing cultural backgrounds for the purpose of creating social change and resolving conflict (Jezewski, 1993). As all the chapters indicate, bridges need to be built more effectively between social service professionals, immigrant families, ethnocultural communities, and the broader society with the goal of achieving equitable access to social services and successful inclusion into societal life. As S. Guo (Chapter 1) identifies, linking with ethnocultural organizations as spaces and places for adult education is a vital way to build social capital across cultural groups and, as Alfred (Chapter 8) calls it, foster global citizenship education that is attentive to the complexities of identity, belonging, and modern-day diasporas. As Gibb (Chapter 5) and Y. Guo (Chapter 4) suggest, legitimating and celebrating plurality of knowledge systems and providing culturally and linguistically accessible community-based learning would be a significant contribution by the field of adult education as well. Considering settlement services as pedagogical spaces and providing capacity-building education for service providers to assist them with the knowledge and emotional challenges of their jobs would also build inclusion. Burstein and Esses (2012) argue that governments "need to create enabling structures to facilitate policy discussion on cross-cutting issues involving settlement agencies and other government ministries" (p. 30).

More research within settlement programming that focuses on adult education and strength-based community development is essential to better understand how to foster welcoming and inclusive communities, within or through challenging restrictive policy and funding regimes. Further, immigrant and refugee communities should be included in program decision-making, thus constituting participatory governance as described by Shan (Chapter 2). For instance, Dobrowolsky and Ramos (2014) support the creation of immigrant advisory councils, which are policy actors and can ensure appropriate gendered perspectives in settlement services.

In the realm of adult education, all the authors have suggested it is imperative that adult educators increase their conversance in migration history and policies, understand colonial and racist mindsets, assess their contradictory roles and implicit deficit thinking, enhance awareness of inclusion/exclusionary dynamics, deconstruct the various discourses around employability and national values, and join together to develop inclusive and critically reflective teaching and learning practices. As Alfred (Chapter 8) describes, a bottom-up approach recognizes individual human capacities and community strengths and is attentive to local social, economic, and ecological justice issues. As Gibb (Chapter 5) and Slade (Chapter 6) offer, reflective adult education practitioners can use "micro-resistances" to avoid complicity in unnecessary retraining, deskilling, standardized and universalized assessments, professional regulatory and credential exclusion, and exploitative volunteer programs while building more positive and culturally respectful alternatives. Joaquin and Johnson-Bailey (Chapter 7) suggest that the field can offer high-quality transnational education of adults that addresses transnational migrant concerns, questions the dynamics of global capital in relation to migration, builds a gendered and critical race analysis to enhance equitable access and participation in adult education, and assists in the goal of creating an immigrant/refugee-positive climate.

By engaging in such practices, the field of adult education can honor the essence of redistributive, recognitive, and representational justice from a transnational perspective, and adult educators have the opportunity to contribute to the co-creation of welcoming communities in which immigrants belong and contribute. In sum, this is what inclusive societies look like.

References

Burstein, M., & Esses, V. (2012). *Study of innovative and promising practices within the immigrant settlement sector.* Ottawa, ON: Canadian Immigrant Settlement Sector Alliance.

Dobrowolsky, A., & Ramos, H. (2014). *Expanding the vision: Why Nova Scotia should look beyond econocentric immigration policy.* Halifax, NS: Canadian Centre for Policy Alternatives Nova Scotia Office.

Fraser, N. (2009). *Scales of justice: Reimagining political space in a globalizing world.* New York, NY: Columbia University Press.

Government of Canada. (2001). *Pursuing Canada's commitment to immigration.* Ottawa, ON: Citizenship and Immigration Canada.

Government of Canada. (2006, March 27). *Moving here, staying here: The Canadian immigrant experience.* Retrieved from https://www.collectionscanada.gc.ca/immigrants /021017-2533.02-e.html

Government of Canada. (2010). *Annual report to Parliament on immigration.* Ottawa, ON: Citizenship and Immigration Canada.

Guo, S. (2010). Toward recognitive justice: Emerging trends and challenges in transnational migration and lifelong learning. *International Journal of Lifelong Education, 29*(2), 149–167.

Hanlon, B., & Vicino, T. (2014). *Global migration: The basics.* London, UK: Routledge.

Jakubowski, L. M. (1997). *Immigration and the legalization of racism.* Halifax, NS: Fernwood.

Jezewski, M. (1993). Culture brokering as a model for advocacy. *Nursing & Health Care: Official Publication of the National League for Nursing, 14*(2), 78–85.

Kelley, N., & Trebilcock, M. (2010). *The making of the mosaic.* Toronto, ON: University of Toronto Press.

Ogilvie, S., & Miller, S. (2006). *Refuge denied: The St. Louis passengers and the Holocaust.* Madison: University of Wisconsin Press.

Simmons, A. (2010). *Immigration and Canada: Global and transnational perspectives.* Toronto, ON: Canadian Scholars' Press Inc.

Stalker, P. (2001). *The no-nonsense guide to international migration.* Toronto, ON: New Internationalist Publications and Between the Lines Press.

Tastsoglou, E., Baillie Abidi, C., Brigham, S., & Lange, E. (2014). (En)gendering vulnerability: Immigrant service providers' perceptions of needs policies and practices related to gender and women refugee claimants in Atlantic Canada. *Refuge, 30*(2), 67–78.

Wayland, S. (2006). *Unsettled: Legal and policy barriers for newcomers to Canada.* Ottawa, ON: Law Commission of Canada and Community Foundations of Canada.

ELIZABETH LANGE is an associate professor in the Department of Adult Education at St. Francis Xavier University, Canada, and is also an associate editor for the Canadian Journal for the Study of Adult Education.

CATHERINE BAILLIE ABIDI is a PhD candidate in the Faculty of Education at St. Francis Xavier University, Canada.

New Directions for Adult and Continuing Education • DOI: 10.1002/ace

INDEX

CPSIA information can be obtained at www.ICGtesting.com
Printed in the USA
BVOW11s0041030316

438855BV00006B/6/P